Living Your Life as a
BEAUTIFUL
OFFERING

A Bible Study Based on the Sermon on the Mount

ANGELA THOMAS

LifeWay Press®
Nashville, Tennessee

Published by LifeWay Press®
© 2004 • Angela Thomas
Sixth Printing July 2010

Derived from the book *A Beautiful Offering*, © 2004 by Angela Thomas
and published with consent of Thomas Nelson Publishers.

ISBN 978-1-4158-2089-6
Item 001260511

Dewey Decimal Classification: 248.843
Subject Headings: CHRISTIAN LIFE \ WOMEN—RELIGIOUS LIFE

Unless otherwise noted, all Scripture quotations are taken from the
Holman Christian Standard Bible®, copyright © 1999, 2000, 2001, 2002, 2003
by Holman Bible Publishers. Used by permission.

Scripture quotations marked NIV are taken from the Holy Bible,
New International Version, copyright © 1973, 1978, 1984 by
International Bible Society. Used by permission.

Scripture quotations marked The Message are taken from The Message,
copyright © 1993, 1994, 1995, 1996, 2000, 2001, 2002 by Eugene Patterson.
Published by NavPress. Used by permission.

Scripture quotations marked RSV are taken from the Revised Standard Version
of the Bible, copyrighted 1946, 1952, © 1971, 1973.

To order additional copies of this resource: WRITE LifeWay Church Resources
Customer Service; One LifeWay Plaza; Nashville, TN 37234-0113;
FAX order to (615) 251-5933; PHONE (800) 458-2772;
ORDER ONLINE at *www.lifeway.com*; E-MAIL *orderentry@lifeway.com*; or
VISIT the LifeWay Christian Store serving you.

Printed in the United States of America

Leadership and Adult Publishing
LifeWay Church Resources
One LifeWay Plaza; Nashville, TN 37234-0175

Contents

ABOUT THE AUTHOR

Angela Thomas is a mother, best-selling author, speaker, and teacher. She is a woman in desperate pursuit of God. Her determination to know God on an intimate level, and her dedication to studying the Bible, have taught her many truths, some discovered through tears and some in times of joy.

Angela graduated from the University of North Carolina at Chapel Hill with a double major in economics and television production. She began full-time work in the field of transportation, but it was her avocation, as part-time youth director, that led her to enroll at Dallas Theological Seminary. She earned her Master's degree in Dallas and moved to North Carolina to become a minister to senior-high girls. Marriage and babies followed not long after, providing Angela with much joy … and much change.

Angela wrote her first book, *Prayers for Expectant Mothers,* during her fourth pregnancy and followed it with *Prayers for New Mothers.* Her 2001 Focus on the Family release, *Tender Mercy for a Mother's Soul,* became a bestseller.

Angela's writing has grown naturally out of her day-to-day life as a mother and as a woman. "I promised God I would tell the truth about my life and His work within me. My writing is just an extension of that. I'm really a storyteller, sharing out of my own life experiences."

Angela's other best-selling writings include *When Wallflowers Dance, Beautiful* (for young women), *Wild About You* (for students), and *Do You Think I'm Beautiful?*

Today, Angela speaks at conferences, retreats, and Bible studies across the country. Audiences enthusiastically respond to her practical, relevant discussions, and she instantly bonds with all types of women. Without the wrappings of pretense or pride, Angela tells it like it is … and how it can be.

Angela and her children, AnnaGrace, William, Grayson, and Taylor, reside in Knoxville, Tennessee. Angela, a single mom, is heavily involved at Two Rivers Church, where her family has attended since moving to Knoxville.

Dear New Friend,

I love the Word of God! I love opening my Bible and reading passage after passage.

I love making notes about fresh ways to understand our timeless God. I love listening to great teaching, and I spend hours every week talking to my best friends about the heart and ways of our Father. I'm so honored to have you join me. I am thrilled that you are doing this study!

I am praying for you as I type these words. I am asking God to let these next weeks be among the most spiritually tender you've ever known. I'm begging Him to give you a willingness and a surrender to the soul work that can happen. I expect God to shout His great love to you. To show you the freedom that awaits inside the strong arms of His protection. To pour out His promised blessings as you lay your life on the altar of His grace.

The one truth that has most profoundly shaped my spiritual life in the past few years is this: the God who knows me fully, loves me still. He pursues me. Rescues me. Delivers me to safety. Defends my reputation. Sets me free. Calls me beautiful. Asks me to dance. I hope you will join me in returning His lavish love with the offering of your life.

I hope you laugh in our sessions together. I hope you learn through the Scriptures and find your heart reminded and encouraged. I want you to meet with God, both in secret and in your circle of friends. I want the truths of the Sermon on the Mount to intersect your everyday life in a very real and astounding way.

Because of Jesus, you and I can live our lives as a beautiful offering. May it be so for your heart and mine.

With great affection,

Angela

ABOUT THE STUDY

Welcome to *Living Your Life as a Beautiful Offering!* By deciding to participate in this study, you are working to return God's love with your life. My prayer for you is that through this study you will find a more passionate life in Christ, a place of rest right in the presence of God, and an understanding that your life—broken, tarnished, ragged, and torn—can still become a beautiful offering.

As you begin your study, keep several things in mind. The material is this book is divided into five days of individual study and is followed by a small-group session every week where you will process with others what you have studied. This is an excellent opportunity to share what the Lord is teaching you as well as learn from what the Lord is teaching other women in your group. If you are studying this material on your own, I encourage you to share what the Lord is showing you with a friend. Each day of individual study should take 20-30 minutes. The personal learning activities are in **bold** print and are designed to help you apply to your life what you are learning. Don't skip over these activities. They will help you get the most from your study. The activities also will prepare you for your small-group session since the leader will ask you to share some of your responses.

Consider the following suggestions to make your study more meaningful.

- Trust the Holy Spirit to be your teacher. Ask Him for guidance as you seek to learn to return your life to Him as a beautiful offering. Release your mind and heart in ready obedience to all He will teach you.
- Pray sincerely both alone and with others. Base your prayers on what the Holy Spirit has revealed to you through your study.
- Keep a spiritual journal of God's activity in your life as well as your response to Him throughout the study. When God speaks, it is important to record it. Your memory will not always recall these "special moments," but your journal will!
- Live out your growing relationship with and knowledge of God in your daily life. Be willing to step out of your comfort zone and share freely with others what the Lord is teaching you.

May God bless you as you seek to dance the dance of your life in His arms!

SESSION ONE ❧ VIEWER GUIDE

Jesus went throughout Galilee, teaching in their synagogues, preaching the good news of the kingdom, and healing every disease and sickness among the people. News about him spread all over Syria, and people brought to him all who were ill with various diseases, those suffering severe pain, the demon-possessed, those having seizures, and the paralyzed, and he healed them. Large crowds from Galilee, the Decapolis, Jerusalem, Judea and the region across the Jordan followed him **(Matthew 4:23-25, NIV).**

> *Blessed are the poor in spirit,*
>   *for theirs is the kingdom of heaven.*
> *Blessed are those who mourn,*
>   *for they will be comforted.*
> *Blessed are the meek,*
>   *for they will inherit the earth.*
> *Blessed are those who hunger and thirst for righteousness,*
>   *for they will be filled.*
> *Blessed are the merciful,*
>   *for they will be shown mercy.*
> *Blessed are the pure in heart,*
>   *for they will see God.*
> *Blessed are the peacemakers,*
>   *for they will be called sons of God.*
> *Blessed are those who are persecuted because of righteousness,*
>   *for theirs is the kingdom of heaven* **(Matthew 5:3-10, NIV).**

The Latin word *beautido* comes from the same root that means _____ .

The Beatitudes can be called the _____ .

There's a difference between the voice of the _____ and the voice of the _____

When you lay yourself on His alter, Jesus' _____ and _____
   make your broken life beautiful.

When he came to his senses, he said, "How many of my father's hired men have food to spare, and here I am starving to death!" **(Luke 15:17).**

When you go to the distant country, it costs _____ you never intended to _____ .

When you come to your senses, turn your _____ toward the _____
and He takes it from there.

A BEAUTIFUL OFFERING

Father, I pray for my sister as she begins this study. Give her a heart of desire. As she opens the pages of Your words to us, please give her a fresh yearning for Your truth.

You are the God of abundance. You are the Giver of gifts. For these weeks, dear God, give her an abundance of spiritual gifts. Pour out your mercy. Welcome Your daughter with open arms.

Father, make these weeks a refuge for her. Give her emotional safety, mental peace, spiritual passion. deeper friendship. Make Your truths poignant and alive to her. Give her wisdom beyond the meager offerings of this teacher. Where there is brokenness, bring healing. Where there is mourning, bring comfort. Where there has been "gotta be," replace it with "when you are." We bring You our everyday lives and all our imperfections. We lay everything we meant to be and everything we want to be at Your feet. Oh Father, make our offering beautiful.

In Jesus' holy name, Amen.

WEEK ONE

Day 1

Come to the Mount

Imagine you've never heard the hymn "Amazing Grace." Pretend you've never read any of the words in the New Testament. No one has ever talked to you about mercy or freedom or being sure you will spend eternity in heaven. You don't know about the Son of God, who has come from a loving Father to be your Savior. There hasn't been a cross or a death or a glorious resurrection.

What if all you've ever known is a spiritual wilderness with rule after rule. A life where you can be shamed for your mistakes, condemned and judged by your peers, even stoned to death as punishment.

Then one day someone tells you about a man traveling through your village. His name is Jesus, and He is making some big claims about where He has come from and to whom He belongs. Some of your friends have seen Him tell a crippled child to stand up and run, and then amazingly, she did. Another person watched Him give calmness to a woman who'd had seizures all her life.

A curious buzz about this man fills the air. One day, a hillside of ordinary folks just like you and me stopped what they were doing to go and meet a man who had come with an extraordinary message. They packed a snack for the kids, closed their shop, or left the flock with a neighbor just to go and hear.

Read Matthew 4:23-25 in the margin and underline the miracles recounted by Matthew.

Why do you think the people came to hear what He had to say that day?

_____

I imagine most of the folks had heard about the miracles. If I were telling someone about this unprecedented man, I'd start with the big stuff too!

What if you had heard about a Creator God, but only the priests inside the temple seemed to have access to Him? You knew sacrifices had to make up for sin and pages and pages of laws had to be kept to please Him. The God of the universe seemed distant and far away, and you weren't ever sure if you could do enough to get to Him or make Him happy. It always felt like God was way up there and you were way down here. Little.

Jesus was going all over Galilee, teaching in their synagogues, preaching the good news of the kingdom, and healing every disease and sickness among the people. Then the news about Him spread throughout Syria. So they brought to Him all those who were afflicted, those suffering from various diseases and intense pains, the demon-possessed, the epileptics, and the paralytics. And He healed them. Large crowds followed Him from Galilee, the Decapolis, Jerusalem, Judea and beyond the Jordan.
Matthew 4:23-25

Insignificant. Almost invisible except for one thing, you had this sinking feeling that God was always mad at you.

When all those people came to hear Jesus they were not drawn to Him because He called down the fire of condemnation or judgment. They dropped what they were doing and followed Him because the miracles proved His authority and His holy compassion drew them in.

When you think about God, where does your mind go first?

❏ righteous judge   ❏ tender heart

❏ condemning critic   ❏ other: _____

List three people who have influenced your thinking toward God.

_____

How have these people shaped your relationship with God?

_____

_____

Do you know the compassionate heart of Jesus personally?
❏ yes   ❏ no

When you speak to someone who doesn't know Jesus, which part of His character do you offer them first, righteous Judge or tender Savior?

_____

Read Matthew 9:36; Mark 8:2; James 5:11 in the margin. Sum up the essence of these passages in one word.

_____

I hope it's been different for you, but I have only come to know this compassionate love of Jesus in the past 10 years. I read those passages, heard with my head, but never truly allowed myself to apply the ideas to my heart. God is changing me and I'm on a mission to tell everyone I can reach about this beautiful, lavish love of God.

When He saw the crowds, He felt compassion for them, because they were weary and worn out, like sheep without a shepherd.
Matthew 9:36

"I have compassion on the crowd, because they've already stayed with Me three days and have nothing to eat."
Mark 8:2

See, we count as blessed those who have endured. You have heard of Job's endurance and have seen the outcome from the Lord: the Lord is very compassionate and merciful.
James 5:11

God is not mad at you because of your humanity. He is fully aware of your limitations, your weaknesses, and the frailties of your heart. His compassion reaches across the heavens to get to you. You have not been cast aside because of your imperfection. Your broken heart is no less precious to Him. Your beauty is not diminished. Your value can never dwindle away.

You are beautiful to God. He has always been taken with you. He wants you to spend the rest of your life in His strong embrace. How will you respond to this amazing, unparalleled kind of love?

I pray that you will respond with your life. Come to the mount and hear the words of Jesus. Observe with your heart why so many were drawn to Him. Believe in His miracles. Feel His compassion. Let Him speak the truth of the kingdom into the everyday moments of your life.

We're going to try on these words of Scripture and learn to allow the grace of God to hold us. I am praying for your heart to unfold, any apprehension or anxiousness to subside, and your spirit to experience a thirst for Jesus.

At various points throughout this study I will encourage you to write your own prayer. When you pray, the Holy Spirit ushers you into the presence of God where your compassionate Jesus is already praying for you. When you pray, there is power. When you pray, you learn to hear from God. When you pray, everything can change.

Start now with a prayer of surrender for the next six weeks. Come to the mount and hear the sermon of Jesus. Ask God to surprise you with fresh teaching, a deeper understanding, and words that give new power to your everyday life. Write your prayer in the margin.

Listen, daughter,
pay attention
and consider:
forget your people
and your father's
house,
and the king will desire
your beauty.
Bow down to him,
for he is your lord
Psalm 45:10-11

DAY 2

WHEN YOU ARE

I usually begin well. I start the day full of energy and enthusiasm. I begin a new project with a big dream and endless resources. This morning I woke with a renewed commitment to holiness and godly living. Good intentions are how I start most everything, but somewhere along the way my humanity usually kicks in.

How would you rate your beginnings?

1	2	3	4	5	6	7	8	9	10

Slow and plodding   **Blasting off like a rocket**

I think I'm super-juggling-power-woman, until I realize I've forgotten to take Taylor to her guitar lesson, all the bills were due two days ago, and I haven't called my best friend in four weeks. Then I'll console myself, "At least I'm operating in godliness, grace, and mercy," until I hear my reaction when one of the children spills wash-out hair color all over the carpet (last night!).

What event or attitude most recently reminded you of your humanity?

_____

Matthew 5:1-12 is the first portion of the Sermon on the Mount—the Beatitudes. Read these verses and complete the chart below listing our human conditions and the blessings offered by our compassionate Lord. The first one has been done for you.

The Condition	The Blessing
poor in spirit	*the kingdom of heaven*

Which blessing appears at the beginning and end of this listing?

_____

Jesus desires that we learn to act and respond like women who belong to the kingdom of God. A theme runs throughout the Sermon on the Mount. Jesus teaches kingdom living for everyday life. For everyday you and everyday me.

We don't have to figure out how to become children of the kingdom. His grace makes it so. What others strive to become, God freely gives. Try to think about this teaching not as a new set of rules or a new standard of morality, but as a new life—a kingdom life offered to you here on earth. Maybe it's the life you've been missing.

As I prayed my way through the Beatitudes, I sensed God was giving me a new insight into these truths. But sometimes I am quick to doubt myself, so I called my favorite seminary professor just to be sure. I jumped in with my quandary, "Jesus begins the Sermon on the Mount with the blessings. Most every time I have heard these taught it felt like I was supposed to become all of these things to receive His approval. Some I am becoming. Some I am trying not to become. And one in particular I have been working hard to avoid all my life. The Beatitudes have felt more like the 'Gotta Be's' to me. Like I 'gotta be' all those things at the same time in the same woman in order to be blessed.

The word blessing *means: approval, encouragement; a thing conducive to happiness or welfare.*[1]

"I feel like the Lord is giving me a new vision of these verses. Would it be accurate if I referred to these blessings as the 'When You Are's?' "

My kind professor assured me that my interpretation was strong. Whew. I could rest in his encouragement and the knowledge that I don't have to be all those things to receive the blessings of God.

Read back through each of the Beatitudes with this new phrasing. Using the following example as a guide.

_____, when you are _____,
  (your name)   (the condition)

Jesus comes with _____.
                  (the blessing)

Which one of these blessings most directly speaks to where you are today? _____

Why? _____

In every circumstance, the connecting link between the condition and the promise is Christ Himself. He stands between our present and our future.

He has opened the kingdom of heaven to all believers. Picture Jesus flinging open the gates of His kingdom just for you. That's exactly what He's doing in these blessings.

Do you see how all this is coming together? Right in the middle of your everyday routine, running carpool, making deadlines, folding laundry, and cooking dinner, Jesus opens the gates of heaven and says, "You can know My blessing. I can make your life a beautiful offering. Just come to Me. Then watch Me stand between your circumstance and the kingdom with My grace."

I am praying that you feel the compassionate presence of Jesus move across heaven and into your everyday routine. I am praying that you hear afresh, or for the first time, His tender voice calling you close.

I sought the LORD,
and He answered me.
Psalm 34:4

As we end today's study, ask Jesus for a real sense of His presence. After you pray, your responsibility is to wait and observe. Specifically pay attention for God's answer. When you know you have heard from God, that He has uniquely answered this prayer, journal His response in the margin.

Sometimes we have not heard the voice of God, afresh or anew, only because we have not asked.

DAY 3

BROKEN

" 'Blessed are the poor
in spirit,
because theirs
is the kingdom
of heaven.' "
Matthew 5:3

I am exhausted. Maybe as empty as I have ever been. Zombie-like. Numb. Physically, mentally, and emotionally baked. I completely hit the wall last Saturday night. I had only been away one night, but it was the weekend after we moved into a new house and the week after I got home from South Africa. Sometimes life crams more into 14 days than a person can absorb.

When it's more than I can take, I cry. That night I drug myself and my luggage into the house sometime after midnight, hugged the baby-sitter, and retucked all my sleeping children. There I was at home, surrounded by my blessings, safe in my bed, just returning from two rewarding days of speaking. And I cried myself to sleep.

Exhaustion seemed to highlight every area of my brokenness. It magnified my frustration over every imperfection. The places this poverty of spirit takes me can be depressing; paralyzing; and overwhelming.

Have you ever known this kind of poverty of spirit? ❑ **yes** ❑ **no**

How does emptiness affect you emotionally?

_____

How does it impact your relationships?

_____

Maybe one of the most frustrating things about being a woman is living inside an invisible ebb and flow of energy and emotion. When I hit the wall, my energy is gone, my heart is flat, and all I can see are my flaws. All I can feel is my poor spirit. I begin to evaluate every area of my life like I'm a failure. I can hear my poor spirit making out a list: _I should bake more and dust more and give more and exercise more and play more and pray more—_ just as I'm falling asleep in my weariness.

When all you can see are the flaws, what do you zero in on first?

_____

When you are spiritually empty and tripping over your failures, how do you think God sees you?

❑ He's mad at me and rolling His heavenly eyes.
❑ He's tired of me asking for forgiveness and strength.
❑ He puts up with me, but He's disappointed.
❑ His love and patience never change.

It's embarrassing to come to Jesus with a poor spirit. I think, _Look at all God has done for me. I should be stronger. I should be an overcomer. I should have renewed energy because of my joy over His love for me. I should be healed by now. More godly by now. Near perfect by now._

What gives me hope is coming to know the heart of Jesus in this passage. When He began to talk to the people about becoming more like the kingdom, He could have said anything like, "Work hard, pray hard, give everything and it probably still won't be enough to please God." Instead, our tender Savior began here, with blessings. In Matthew 5:3, we can see for ourselves that there is blessing for the poor in spirit.

According to the verses at the top of page 16, what does God do for the brokenhearted?

Psalm 34:18 _____

Psalm 147:3 _____

Isaiah 61:1 _____

Maybe, like me, you really need to deal with your desperate heart. Maybe you're not in this place just now, but you'll need to know what to do the next time your spirit is poor and your brokenness is as bright as a neon sign.

Here is the answer. Here is the way toward blessing: Lay your broken, poor spirit on the altar of God. Here's what I mean, step-by-step:

1. *Figure out where you are.*

Sometimes you have to get away from the daily spin to be able to see. You may need some quiet moments or places to begin where you are.

Psalm 32:3-8

As you begin to take inventory of your spirit, check the statements that describe where you are.

❑ I feel myself smiling, but I'm empty underneath the smile.
❑ My heart is willing, but my body is tired.
❑ My heart is broken, and it keeps breaking in all the same places.
❑ I have made too many commitments, and I'm overwhelmed.

Psalm 34:4-7

❑ I have separated myself from everyone, and I am lonely.
❑ My wounds are taking forever to heal.
❑ I'm just really, really lost.

2. *Take the truth of where you are and lift it to heaven.*

Psalm 34:17-20

When I give an attitude, a sin, or my brokenness to God, I come to Him in prayer, usually timid at first and mostly embarrassed that I still have this stuff to deal with. Sometimes I lie on my floor and pray through my tears. Sometimes I write out my prayers in my journal. Sometimes I pray outloud in the car while I'm driving. However it happens, what is important is that my poor spirit is turned toward God. What is inward is being turned upward, handed over to my heavenly Father.

Psalm 38:5-22

Read the words of David from the Psalms passages listed in the margin and write the promises God makes to one who is wrestling through his or her own humanity.

David models for us over and over the power of truth before God. Write your own prayer of truth. You may need to step out of your comfort zone and say things to God that you've never voiced.

_____

_____

I pray that as you speak to God you will find a deeper intimacy with Him. I want you to know a freedom that only comes from openness. I want you to begin to desire this kind of exchange with God. When your spirit is poor, I want you to desire the presence of God instead of the shadows of loneliness or the distraction of sin.

Day 4

Pressing Deeper Still

Sometimes when I am feeling especially broken or attacked or poured out, I will joke with my friends, "I don't know about this deeper walk with God, maybe I just want to be shallow." Wanting to be shallow is funny and we have a good laugh, but it's not true. I know what shallow feels like. I see what shallow looks like. I don't want to skim across the surface with God. There is no life or passion in the shallow heart.

Yesterday I told you that God wants your broken spirit. He wants you to come into His presence and lay all the pieces of your heartache on His altar. He promises to cover the offering of your brokenness with the blessing of His kingdom. I began outlining some baby steps for us to take. Let's pick up with number 3.

3. Talk about where you are to someone who is safe.

I realize some of you just checked out. Try to stay with me in this idea of community and friendship. I recently read something that was powerful:

"People _heal_ in authentic, God-centered relationships and families— and people without these resources recover much more slowly, if at all."[2]

Although the following information speaks to the results of a national task force study of how students grow in their faith, I think there is something here for us as well: "Three professional experiences [brought] one striking conclusion: Students _grow in their faith through relationships,_

I am afflicted
and needy; …
You are my help
and my deliverer,
my God, do not delay.
Psalm 40:17

wounded people heal in relationships, and unbelievers come to the Lord through relationships."[3]

Write Galatians 6:2 in the margin.

Who is on standby in your circle of friendship or community to help you carry your burden?

_____

Are you willing to let them in?
❏ yes   ❏ no   ❏ I'm willing to try.

One of the most difficult things for me is to let other people into the back room of my brokenness. It's embarrassing, so I hesitate. Then my pride jumps in and makes things worse. I have mistakenly believed I can become strong enough to get healthy alone. I have even acted like I could trust God enough to heal all by myself. What a desperately foolish idea.

Broken hearts and broken lives don't get put back together while you're laying on your bed in the dark. They get healed inside the arms of healthy love.

You and I were made for relationship. We are supposed to live in community with loving people. Burdens are meant to be carried. Broken hearts and broken lives don't get put back together while you're laying on your bed in the dark. They get healed inside the arms of healthy love.

Think about a time you experienced healing. How did it come to you?

_____

Who was instrumental to the process?

_____

Looking back, how can you see God's hand in that journey?

_____

I have a prayer team I e-mail about once a week. These people stand underneath the burdens of my life with me and rejoice in every good thing beside me. It does no good to have a prayer team if I don't tell them the truth. Here's an e-mail I sent last week:

Hello my friends,
I realize you can't pray in power unless I tell the truth …

I completely hit the wall of emptiness and exhaustion last Saturday night. On the way home from Pennsylvania the meltdown was inevitable. I cried myself to sleep and slept off and on for the next few days. I am exhausted, physically and emotionally. I am tired of being "a really strong woman who can get it all done." I am tired of feeling like I have to live like I don't need anybody but Jesus. Can you pray into the loneliness that comes from so many blessings and no one to share both the responsibilities and the joy?

I have only had a prayer team for a year and a half. But I can pinpoint to the month a literal turning toward growth in my ministry, family, and heart. It began when I asked people to pray for me. Why do we wait so long to ask?

4. Wait.

Healing takes time. There will never be just 12 steps to healing. You cannot microwave something that God has designed to bake slowly in the heart. To choose healing is to lay your brokenness on the altar of God. There could be a hundred more healthy things you can do in this process, but you cannot factor out time. You cannot circumvent what happens when you learn to wait in the presence of God.

5. Learn everything you can.

I truly believe that one of the best things I carry into my future ministry and relationships is my brokenness. When you know what it feels like to be blown into a million pieces and then picked up and held by the tenderness of God, something happens in that transaction of grace. You want to give what you have received.

I want to love with a pure love, because I have received it in abundance. I want to forgive like crazy because it has been given to me. I want to get people into the presence of God where the Father makes all things new. I want to tell people they can dance again because God said we can dance in His arms for His glory.

According to 2 Corinthians 4:7-18, what treasure has God given you because of brokenness?

_____

_____

I waited and waited
and waited for God.
At last he looked;
 finally he listened.
He lifted me out
 of the ditch,
 pulled me from
 deep mud.
He stood me up on
 a solid rock
 to make sure
 I wouldn't slip.
He taught me how
 to sing the latest
 God-song,
 a praise-song
 to our God.
More and more people
 are seeing this:
 they enter the
 mystery,
 abandoning
 themselves to God.
Psalm 40:1-3,
The Message

What happens to the one who lays her heart on the altar of God (vv. 8-9)?

_____ but not _____

_____ but not _____

_____ but not _____

_____ but not _____

What is the benefit of your brokenness and heartache (v. 15)?

_____

Therefore, do not _____ (v. 16).
In and through our struggle, what is happening in the unseen?

(vv. 17-18)? _____

Thank God for the treasure He makes from your heartache.

DAY 5

HOLY COMFORT

" 'Blessed are those who mourn, because they will be comforted.' "
Matthew 5:4

When I was 14, my only sister drowned and my soul mourned. My aunt was killed in a plane crash two years later and our whole family returned to that dark place filled with spiritual questions and aching. But during my divorce, I stepped onto a path that took me into the deepest midnight I have ever known. I call it a path, but in truth, it felt like I had been strapped inside a rocket ship, whirling out of control toward the edge of nothing, alone.

The uncertainty of those days made the weight of pain so thick I thought I would surely suffocate. I remember being surprised every morning I woke up and found myself still breathing.

We cry over loss and disappointment. We lament the way life wasn't supposed to turn out. At first, it's okay to weep openly and brush a few tears away. Eventually it seems like enough time has passed, even though it hasn't, so we smile politely, pretend we've healed, and run home to ache all alone.

People have good hearts. They mean well. They want to say something profound. Something to ease the pain. Something spiritual. Something to make all the hurt go away. They lob out a few things they heard someone else say and those well-meaning words land like bricks in your heart.

"Angela, just think about how many people you'll be able to connect with because of the heartache you're going through." *I don't want to connect with anybody. Why can't I connect over gourmet cooking or raising preschoolers or exercise class? Who the heck would ever choose pain for connection?*

"These trials will make you stronger." *I don't want to be strong. I want to be carried like a little baby. Protected. Naïve. Sheltered.*

"God will receive glory in your suffering." *I promise I will give God the glory if we can just skip this whole thing.*

Think of a time of mourning in your life. What were the most powerful words spoken to you?

_____

What words left you empty?

_____

I love all the people in my life for trying. A lot of people hung in there and kept coming back every time I pushed them away. They have carried, bandaged, loved, and held me through so many seasons of mourning. There is a people-love that God sends to begin the healing, but eventually there is a God-love that breaks through with holy comfort. The blessing of laying your mourning on God's altar is that He will come with a divine comfort only He can give.

> *Ultimately, mourning means facing what wounds us in the presence of One who can heal.*
>
> —Henri Nouwen[4]

My friend said to me one day, "I don't think you know your Bible too well. God says we 'walk through the valley of the shadow of death.'" (Psalm 23). My friend was right. I had forgotten. It felt like I had bought a house in the valley of the shadow and I was doomed to live there for the rest of my days. Even though movement seemed imperceptible, God was carrying me through this valley and into the promised land of His healing.

Why would a rod and staff comfort? "The rod conveys the concept of authority, of power, of discipline, of defense against danger. The staff is essentially a symbol of the concern, the compassion that a shepherd has for his charges. No other single word can better describe its function on behalf of the flock than that it is for their comfort. The word 'staff' speaks of all that is longsuffering and kind."[5]

God is moving to take you toward a divine, holy comfort. How have you known the comfort of God?

_____

Even though I walk
* through*
the valley of the shadow
* of death,*
I will fear no evil,
for you are with me;
your rod and your staff,
* they comfort me.*
Psalm 23:4, NIV

I only have these eyes and this heart to process with, but here are some of the characteristics of holy comfort that I have come to know:

1. When God breaks through with His God-comfort, I can finally get my next breath. (See Jeremiah 31:13.)

2. I am able to surrender my life and my outcome into His strong arms. I realize I am surrendered when I hear those around me fret about my circumstances and my heart is still fully at peace. I know God is working when old thought patterns race through my mind, but they don't take hold and grip me with fear anymore. (See Revelation 21:3-4.)

3. In spite of outward suffering or inevitable conclusions, a deep and abiding rest has come into my heart. What matters most has been given its rightful priority. Love matters. Integrity matters. Peace matters. Fairness isn't as important as it once was. What others might think seems to fade into a mist. (See Psalm 91:1-2.)

4. I can begin to trace God's hand across the events of my life. Squinting maybe, but I'm beginning to see that He is present and His promises are real. (See 2 Samuel 22:31-37.)

5. Hope has a new name and He is called faithful God, my sovereign Lord, King of the universe—the One who comes to rescue broken little girls like me and you. (See Lamentations 3:19-26.)

Where do you need to know the comfort of God in your life?

_____

Which of these verses speaks most profoundly to your circumstances and why? Write your answer in the margin.

---

1 Frederick C. Mish, editor-in-chief, *Merriam-Webster's Collegiate Dictionary; Tenth Edition* (Springfield, MA: Merriam-Webster, Inc., 2002), 122.

2 James G Friesen, E. James Wilder, Anne M. Bierling, Rick Koepche, and Maribeth Poole, *The Life Model—Living from the Heart Jesus Gave You: The Essentials of Christian Living* (Pasadena: Shepherd's House, Inc., 2000), 5.

3 Ibid.

4 Henri Nouwen, *Turn My Mourning into Dancing* (Word Publishing: Nashville, 2001), xv.

5 Phillip Keller, *A Shepherd Looks at Psalm 23* (Grand Rapids: Zondervan, 1970), 97.

SESSION TWO ❧ VIEWER GUIDE

Blessed are those who hunger and thirst for righteousness,
for they will be filled (Matthew 5:6).

Long before he laid down earth's foundations, he had us in mind, had settled on us as the focus of his love, to be made whole and holy by his love. Long, long ago he decided to adopt us into his family through Jesus Christ. (What pleasure he took in planning this!)
(Ephesians 1:4-5, The Message).

When you feel empty, God is calling you to be _____

and _____ for His righteousness.

The _____ you love cannot make you whole.

Your _____ cannot make you whole.

Accumulating _____ will not make you whole.

To become hungry for Jesus:

1. _____ God to make it so.

2. _____ yourself into His presence anyway.

The sluggard craves and gets nothing,
but the desires of the diligent are fully satisfied (Proverbs 13:4).

3. Ask others to _____ for you.

4. Get around others who are _____.

5. Let go of false _____ and expect

_____.

6. _____ on God.

THE CUP OF YOUR SOUL

Father, Sometimes in the spin of life, we just

forget. We forget to ask for the deeper

life. We forget to drink and eat of Your

righteousness. We forget what is

priority, what matters most, what

feeds the soul.

Please remind us to ask for hunger and thirst. Remind us to be deliberate in our intention. Teach us that this desire could make the difference in all our spiritual pursuit.

Draw us deeper into Your Word. Teach us truths that will begin to change our everyday lives for Your glory. Show us how to look more and more like You, less and less like we have. Highlight every hindrance that needs to be removed. Give us courage and strength as we bring our emptiness and ask for Your filling.

God, please bless my sister this week. Show her what it feels like to become spiritually and emotionally full of Your presence. Remove every distraction that could keep her from seeking You. Give peace to her daily life.

In the name of Jesus, Amen.

WEEK TWO ❧

Day 1

Just Who You Are

When I was a new mom I felt insecure around moms who seemed to know exactly what every cry meant. It took me at least 12 variations of walking, rocking, and patting to figure out how to soothe my newborn. It would have been great if the same thing had always worked, but it never did. For at least a year I felt like I wasn't a very good mom. How can one instinctively know that a 4 month old wants to listen to light jazz with the bathroom light on, the bedroom door partially cracked, content that her mom is outside in the hallway, face down, begging Jesus to put her to sleep?

When my firstborn was in kindergarten, I felt stupid all over again wondering, *How did all the other moms know that you tape a piece of candy to kindergarten Valentine cards before you send them to school?* I was probably the only dorky mom who just sent the cards that Taylor had scribbled her name on the night before. Some moms even made cute little bags stuffed with an assortment of candy and toys, tied with beautiful ribbons. Where do they learn this stuff? There should be a class or something!

Many times I have felt I wasn't smart enough, witty enough, skinny enough, spiritual enough, probably not enough of anything that matters.

God is not surprised by our insecurities. He wants to use us anyway.

Is there an area where God has been calling you but you're dragging your feet, feeling like you're not enough? If yes, what is it?

_____

In the following paragraphs, underline words and phrases that define *meekness*. Circle false ideas of meekness.

When Jesus said there is a blessing for the meek, I didn't get it at first. I thought of meekness more as false humility, aloof and unassuming. That fake thing we do sometimes to downplay our accomplishments or how hard we worked to achieve a goal. I have come to realize Jesus was saying that when you are meek you are well acquainted with your own flaws. The meek realize they will never be enough and recognize they will always need a Savior to complete them.

The meek are uncomfortable with their inadequacy because it's very humbling to realize "it's just me." And yet that's the very place where Jesus can step in with His strength and give the blessing.

" 'Blessed are the meek, for they will inherit the earth.' "
Matthew 5:5, NIV

Definitions of meek:

Greek: *gentle, meek, the positive moral quality of dealing with people in a kind manner, with humility and consideration*

Hebrew: *humble, afflicted, poor, oppressed*

When we lay our meekness on God's altar, we say something like this:

God, today it's just me, part of the way there, but so much further to go. It's just me in both my desire and my weakness. It's just the woman You made, still in process, not yet the woman You must have envisioned. Show Yourself to me today. Please take this offering and make everything I'm not more than enough because You live inside me.

Based on what you just read, fill in the chart below.

Meekness is …	Meekness is not …

Whom do I have in heaven but You? And I desire nothing on earth but You. My flesh and my heart may fail, but God is the strength of my heart, my portion forever.
Psalm 73:25-26

Sometimes when we consider meekness, we imagine a person lacking confidence or backbone. In fact, Jesus wants to give the meek a go-get-'em, inherit-the-earth kind of confidence. He is our Savior, our Completer, the One who takes our pieces and makes them whole. He takes our weak effort and makes it powerful. He is our covering.

Can you picture "the covering of Christ" in your mind? Imagine curling up in the strong arms of Jesus. His shoulders curve in tenderness around your tired body. His head is bent low so that His cheek brushes against your tear-stained face. His hand gently strokes your hair. You feel His power. You are protected. You are safe. Because you are within Christ's strength you too become strong. Nothing can have you. You belong to God.

When you and I lay our lives on the altar of God, we put ourselves inside the covering of Christ. It's there that He takes meek women and makes them amazing.

When we are sure we are not enough, in desperate need of the Savior's strength, then our lives become beautiful offerings, because God comes to the rescue with all the resources of His kingdom here on earth.

I pray that He may grant you, according to the riches of His glory, to be strengthened with power through His Spirit in the inner man, and that the Messiah may dwell in your hearts through faith.
Ephesians 3:16-17

Read Psalm 73:25-26 and Ephesians 3:16-17 in the margin and fill in the blanks.

God is the _____ of my heart, my _____ forever.

Be _____ with power through His Spirit.

When you question God's love for you and your questions make you insecure, read Isaiah 54:10 and Ephesians 3:17-19 and ask God for His assurance of love. It's okay to ask for more than enough—to be filled to the measure of all fullness.

When you find yourself afraid, in need of His love or His presence to overcome your fears, read Psalm 4:8. As a single mom, alone at night, when all the fears seem to pound on my door, this verse is powerful to me.

Read these passages in the margin and match them to the message from each.

Isaiah 54:10   We live in peace and safety.

Ephesians 3:17-19   His love will never be removed from us.

Psalm 4:8   We are filled with the fullness of God's love.

When we feel we are not enough, the covering of Christ makes us more. When we hide our meekness in the shadows or back away from God because of our lack or inability, we are living outside the covering of Christ. It's okay not to be enough, because we are made to need Him. He is enough every time we are not.

How can you have that kind of faith? You choose to believe that God is who He said He is, Jesus is His Son, and that His death paid for your sins. You choose to accept by faith that it's all true. You decide to put your burden down and rest in God as your Father and Jesus as your Savior.

Have you learned to put your burden down and rest in the Lord? If you're having difficulty, write a prayer in the margin asking God to help you have this kind of faith. Be honest with Him about what you're feeling right now.

God knows it's just you and He knows it's just me. He sent a Savior to make us whole and to make us strong and to make us enough. Hide yourself in His arms today. Let Him make your meager offering beautiful. Feel the strength of His protection. Hear the whisper of His promise to you …

"There is an inheritance on earth, and it belongs to the woman in My arms."

*"Though the mountains move
and the hills shake,
My love will not be
removed from you
and My covenant of
peace will not be
shaken,"
says your compassionate
L*ORD*.*
Isaiah 54:10

I pray that you, being rooted and firmly established in love, may be able to comprehend with all the saints what is the breadth and width, height and depth, and to know the Messiah's love that surpasses knowledge, so you may be filled with all the fullness of God.
Ephesians 3:17-19

*I will both lie down and sleep in peace,
for You alone, L*ORD*,
make me live in safety.*
Psalm 4:8

DAY 2

HUNGRY AND THIRSTY
FOR RIGHT LIVING

Love hurts. I wish it didn't, but human love can wear us out. We're fickle and we play games. We say, "Come close, now go away." Many of us have been burned so many times by people we love that love isn't very appealing anymore. It's scary. It requires trust. The heart could get broken again. The one we love might run away or turn away.

Kids stop talking to their parents. Married people end up only sharing the same air. Friends grow apart. It's all such a shame because every person I know has room for more love—a soul of emptiness just waiting to be filled. But the older we get, the more hesitant we are. Reluctant to dive in head first. Afraid of being tricked. It can never be like a romance novel or a storybook family. Real love is hard and a lot of work and, we've come to believe, inevitably disappointing. Personally, I taught my heart to go numb, so I wouldn't feel the pain.

I have friends who've been married 52 years. They raised 5 children together and lost another to death. They live in a retirement village with other folks their age and do everything together. They are still best friends.

He chauffeurs her to the mall and waits patiently for her to try on shoes or find a new lipstick. She wipes his chin when mayonnaise drips from his sandwich and makes sure his shirts are pressed just the way he likes them. They send each other cards. Leave each other notes. And hold hands like they just met. She still laughs at his old jokes, and he still calls her Baby. I watch them lean into each other affectionately and admire their mutual desire for one another.

One day I asked her, "How did you keep your relationship strong?"

She said, "We just kept falling in love."

The God of heaven is inviting us to keep falling in love with Him. To His invitation He attaches the promise of a blessing. It's the blessing we've been craving, the one we've all been looking for. When you and I desire God more than anything, when we commit with our lives to keep falling in love, He comes and fills up our hearts.

Examine your heart for any numbness, places where you can't feel anymore. What makes you hesitant about love?

_____

Here's the motivator and reason to take this seriously—in your pursuit of Him, God promises what you've always wanted and what you cannot get anywhere else on earth—a full heart.

" 'Blessed are those who hunger and thirst for righteousness, because they will be filled' " (Matt. 5:6). We live in a society where most of us never hunger or thirst for anything. We never allow ourselves to physically experience either one. We drive through a fast-food restaurant just before we think we might have a hunger pang. So this idea of feeling desperate for food or drink already seems weird.

To hunger or thirst means to have an eager desire; to crave urgently; long; desire with one's whole heart. For the hungry and the thirsty, being filled becomes the number one priority.

Righteousness is the right living that comes out of your desire for God. To hunger and thirst for the righteousness of God is to desire Him more than anything. It is longing for His consistent presence and His input in your life, just like your consistent need for food. When you continually feel hunger and thirst, you keep coming back to your priority. You keep looking to be fed and you keep looking for God. In the process, you keep falling in love.

> Right living *means that we begin to desire what God desires. It means that our longings begin to line up with His purposes and His plans. Our decisions get filtered through the grid of His instruction, our love begins to mirror the reflection of His love for us, and our motives are refined as we consider His will.*

What did Jesus say to the church of Ephesus in Revelation 2:4?

You have forsaken your _____   _____.

Maybe you find yourself without a passionate love for God, wondering if there is more. Maybe you have never known great thirst or hunger for the right living of God or maybe your soul has fallen asleep, not even realizing that your stomach is growling for His fullness. Wherever you find yourself, let's find our way together toward His righteousness and His blessing.

Which words best describe your relationship with God right now.

- ❑ asleep, snoring, not even aware of God around me
- ❑ disinterested and unmotivated
- ❑ wanting more but feeling unsure about what to do, inconsistent
- ❑ walking toward God, sometimes distracted
- ❑ running toward a God life, desperate to know Him more

How do you think you could increase your hunger for God?

_____

Do your answers seem to involve more ❑ rules or more ❑ freedom? Check one.

What activities or people give you energy and make you excited?

_____

Which people, circumstances, studies, music, or interactions have given you a renewed spiritual energy and enthusiasm for God in the past?

_____

*God, create a clean heart for me
and renew a steadfast spirit within me.
Do not banish me from Your presence
or take Your Holy Spirit from me.
Restore the joy of Your salvation to me,
and give me a willing spirit.*
Psalm 51:10-12

When I am empty or without spiritual hunger, if I can come alongside someone who desires God, then I feel my spirit being renewed in their presence. There is a woman who comes about once a month to help me knock the dust off this house. We usually work together for a few hours and try to restore some order to the chaos. Her name is Beverly, and I can't wait to see her every time. This woman comes through the door with the words of Jesus on her lips. She sings praise songs. She prays all through my house—at every entrance, in the children's rooms. A couple of months ago we spent our cleaning time with me on my knees and Beverly calling down heaven on my behalf. After I have been with this spiritual giant, my heart is renewed. My spirit longs for more of God. She has sloshed out Jesus and made me thirsty. You pace yourself according to whom you run beside.

When you lean in, God bends down to lift you up. When you ask for hunger and thirst, He comes to make you full. Maybe, like me, you forget to ask for spiritual desire. Don't let any more time pass. Life is a beautiful offering when you are crying out for God to come and make you hungry for His righteousness, because He is the only One who will satisfy your spiritual appetite with the food that can fill your soul.

Stop whatever is going on and pray something like this:

God, make me hungry and thirsty for You. Give me a desire for right living that takes priority over everything else in my life. Then, God, come with the blessing of a full heart. I want to live and love from Your fullness. Take my offering and make it beautiful. Carry me to the next level with You. I love You. I want to love You more. Amen.

DAY 3

THE HINDRANCE OF LAZY

Last night after dinner, my 10-year-old son, Grayson, came into the kitchen and asked, "Can I mow the yard?"

Never having heard that question from one of my children, I asked, "Come again?"

"Can I mow the yard?"

"Well, sure you can. The mower is under the house and it probably needs some gas." I wanted to see if his mowing vision waned in the light of a few obstacles.

"Okay," he said, skipping out the door, leaving his dumbfounded mother leaning over the sink.

He lugged the mower from under the house, but couldn't crank it. Cranking yard tools is usually a family effort. Grayson holds the bar down, I pull the starter rope until my arm is rubber, and AnnaGrace prays. She always paces and prays when I have to crank the mower. Probably overspiritualizing, but every time she gets God involved, the thing starts.

Anyway, we didn't have enough gas, so I put everybody in the car to run to the gas station, and, eventually, we got it all going. Then that little guy mowed the yard like a professional. No whining. No stopping every other lap for more water. I kept coming outside to check on him, partly because of my proud mother's heart and partly waiting for his mower legs to wear out and for him to motion for me to take over.

He would yell to me over the roar, "Why are you watching me?" like he's asked to mow a million times, and I'd laugh.

Then an even weirder thing happened. Grayson's eight-year-old brother, William, said, "I want to mow."

"Huh?"

"Can I mow the back yard?"

"Sure, honey, as soon as Grayson is done in the front."

Then big shot William mowed the back yard not once, but twice— "just for fun." One time long ways and the second time, kind of diagonal.

"It's perfect," I told him.

While the boys mowed, I edged and swept and blew off the driveway. We worked until we couldn't see another thing on that humid July night. We were sweaty and thirsty and nasty dirty. But it felt good to work hard together. So good in fact that William wanted to shoot off the rest of his firecrackers to celebrate our great yard. So we did. Nine loud bangs. Hooray for hard work!

Later that night I was thinking about being hungry and thirsty for right living. I realized I have never run in the door to God and asked, "Can I mow the yard for you?" It has never occurred to me to ask God,

Would You give me a willing heart to do the stuff no one else wants to do?
Will You let me do a job that's bigger than me?
Give me energy even when I am inconvenienced by the obstacles.
Please let me get sweaty and messy and tired.
Make me uncomfortably hungry and thirsty for You.
And God, while I'm mowing or whatever, don't let me be a whiney-baby.

Some of us might as well be lying on the sofa, flipping through the cable channels for God. Cushy spirituality. Maybe even spiritually lazy or asleep, avoiding anything that might require effort or discipline or muscle.

Have you ever asked God if you could "mow the yard"?
❑ yes ❑ no

How long since you asked God for something challenging?

_____

How about discipline? Are you in training and building spiritual muscles or lying around snacking in front of the TV?

_____

"Up on your feet! Take a deep breath! Maybe there's life in you yet. But I wouldn't know it by looking at your busywork; nothing of God's work has been completed. Your condition is desperate. Think of the gift you once had in your hands, the Message you heard with your ears—grasp it again and turn back to God."
Revelation 3:2-3,
The Message

Take a look at what is written to the church at Sardis in Revelation 3:2-3 (in the margin). Sometimes life spins us around and makes us crazy. The survival/sleepless years with babies and toddlers. Sickness. Three jobs. Limited finances. Divorce. We can find ourselves spiritually weary. I have lived there. I think God understands and gives grace in differing seasons.

But sometimes we just get lazy. Some events in our lives have even come to shake our souls awake. The alarm is blaring and we just keep hitting the snooze button.

As I think about the hindrances to spiritual desire or becoming hungry and thirsty for God, one of the most glaring is the tendency to get lazy. We'll talk about the other tomorrow.

I've said a million times, "If I could only buy discipline." In the same way, we cannot buy spiritual desire. It requires a choice. I have to choose to move toward what I am not, learning, persisting, and wanting until I become.

What could you do to move toward what God wants you to become? Check all that apply.

- ❏ be willing to step out of my comfort zone to serve God
- ❏ ask God to help me regain my spiritual desire
- ❏ view obstacles as opportunities rather than inconveniences
- ❏ pull the covers over my head and hope things look better in the morning
- ❏ other: _____

A full heart and a full life with God involves a choice.

Will you choose to do whatever it takes to get hungry and thirsty?
❏ yes ❏ no

If yes, write a prayer in the margin asking God to help you recapture your spiritual desire.

*How long will you stay
 in bed, you slacker?
When will you get up
 from your sleep?
A little sleep, a little
 slumber,
a little folding of the
 hands to rest,
and your poverty will
 come like a robber,
your need, like a bandit.*
Proverbs 6:9-11

Day 4

The Hindrance of Doubt

Doubting God will completely paralyze our faith. How can we hunger for what we aren't sure we believe? If we are operating with an uncertainty about God, then in our weakest moments we have nothing to guide our choices. Nothing to anchor the heart. Nothing on which to build a strong life.

Doubt can blow through our heads like a thought out of nowhere, but we can also let doubt come in and take up a lot of space in our hearts. Doubt reflects a mistrust because of questions or unbelief.

Have you ever struggled with spiritual doubt? About what issues?

_____

Whenever a question about God comes to me out of nowhere, the most powerful thing I can do is recite to myself what I know to be true about God. When we apply scriptural truths to our lives, the light of God is faithful to chase doubt away. Let's walk through some truths together.

Read from your Bible each verse listed below. Write some thoughts about what the attribute means to you.

God is *sovereign*. God is in control. He holds all people, time, and circumstances in the palm of His hand.
1 Samuel 2:6-10   1 Chronicles 29:11-12   Psalm 24:1   Romans 8:28
I believe God's sovereignty is:

_____

God is *unchangeable*. He cannot be less than He is. He does not vary. His knowledge and holiness do not change.
Numbers 23:19   Psalm 102:27   Malachi 3:6   James 1:17
I believe God's unchangeability is:

_____

God is *omnipresent*. God is not restricted by space or time. He is always with us in every place and circumstance.
Jeremiah 23:23-24   Psalm 73:23-24   Psalm 139:7-12
I believe God's omnipresence is:

_____

God is *omnipotent*. God is all-powerful. He can do whatever He wills and His holiness directs His perfect will.
Psalm 147:5   Luke 1:37   Ephesians 3:20
I believe God's omnipotence is:

_____

God is *truth*. He is faithful. If He says it, it will come to pass.
Numbers 23:19   Isaiah 45:19   John 14:6   Revelation 3:14
I believe God's truthfulness is:

_____

God is *good*. He gives mercy and grace from His goodness. He cares about all His created and their welfare.
Psalm 34:8   Psalm 100:5   Mark 10:18   Ephesians 2:4-5

I believe God's goodness is:

_____

God is _just_. He has absolute authority. God doesn't play favorites and He makes His justice available to all.
Psalm 99:1-4   1 John 1:9
I believe God's justice is:

_____

God is _love_. He is the unfailing source of all love. Love is His primary motive. All creation has been formed to satisfy His love.
John 3:16   1 John 4:8-16
I believe God's love is:

_____

God is _holy_. He is right in all His ways. He hates what is evil and is devoted to what is good.
1 Samuel 2:2   Isaiah 6:3   Isaiah 57:15   Revelation 15:4
I believe God's holiness is:

_____   _____

Sometimes we trivialize God. We throw up a few "bless me" prayers without giving a second thought to who is really listening. I need to stop every so often and let God's grandeur overwhelm me. When I am overwhelmed by His glory, my heart wants to bow down and worship. My doubt washes away. His perfection and love affirm my commitment to Christ.

When I remember that God is Creator and I am created, God is perfect and I am flawed, God is pure love and I am fickle, God is good and loves me anyway, I rest and find strength in committing my life to His glory.

What have these truths done for any doubts you had?

_____

DAY 5

ANYTHING THAT KEEPS YOU FROM GOD

Two nights ago I woke up at 3:53 a.m. It wasn't one of those roll-over-and-squint-at-the-clock moments, it was an instant jolt from a dead sleep. A middle-of-the-night, think-about-your-life kind of reveille. A maybe-you-should-pray kind of stirring.

I began to pray. Praise. A pure heart. My children. God's provision. My parents. Our protection. Random, 4:00 a.m. praying. I was without a focused direction, but very sure of the prompting. I don't know how long I prayed, but, eventually, I stumbled into this question, *God, did You wake me to tell me something?* I heard God's answer so clearly in my mind, *Step away from everything that tries to hurt you.*

Almost immediately I understood exactly what God was saying. I felt obligated to maintain relationships with certain Christian men and women in my life whose friendships hurt. These people didn't treat me with kindness. Their confusing words and actions were unhealthy. I knew God was saying, *Step away.* In the dark of my room, God woke me up, turned on every light in my heart, and for a few moments gave me eyes to see what I had not been able to see before.

How does God usually "wake you up"? Check all that apply.

- ❑ through others
- ❑ through His Word
- ❑ through sermons
- ❑ through music
- ❑ through prayer
- ❑ other: _____

This week we have been talking about hindrances to hunger and thirst. So much about our everyday lives with God hinges on our desire for right living. If we find ourselves apathetic, for whatever reason, then we haven't moved toward God. He is the One who adds power to our ordinary, the Father who runs to dance with His beloved, the Almighty who knows the number of hairs on your head and the needs in your heart.

Invite God to do whatever it takes to get your attention. Give Him permission to hold an early morning prayer meeting or stop you on the street and speak through a stranger. Take a minute to get rid of any preconceived ideas about how you will hear from God.

Let's look at a few more hindrances to desiring God.

1. Is there a person(s) in your life, even at church, who "speaks death" to you? Do they tear down more than they build up? Does this relationship distract or hinder you from growing in your desire for God? Scripture refers to these people as foolish and advises us to stay away.

Read the passages from Proverbs in the margin. On the lines below, write the characteristics of a fool listed in each passage.

Proverbs 13:19 _____

Proverbs 14:9 _____

Proverbs 14:16 _____

Without writing down names, ask God very specifically if foolish people have been speaking into your life. What is the instruction from Scripture regarding these people? (See Proverbs 14:7.)

_____

2. Even though I may be growing up in Christ, my sin is also evolving. I still have stuff to deal with, it's just different than it used to be. In maturity, sin can become less blatant, more hidden, and even accepted in some weird way

I can usually see the big stuff coming—drunkenness, sexual immorality, legalism, hatred, disunity, etc.—and run away. But sin is deceptive and never stops trying to work its way in. Some of the things I have dealt with in my spiritual growing up are things that quietly do damage to my soul.

A jaded heart. After a while I realized that no one or nothing impressed me anymore. It actually felt cool to be so jaded. It's not cool. It's haughty and God has severely dealt with me in this.

Apathy. We all have days of greater or less compassion and enthusiasm. That's not what I mean. We can grow apathetic toward people, our own lives, our spiritual condition, and eventually grow cold toward God. Remember the church in Laodicea?

"I know your works, that you are neither cold nor hot. I wish that you were cold or hot. So, because you are lukewarm, and neither hot nor cold, I am about to vomit you out of My mouth" (Rev. 3:15-16).

Comparison. I guess this could be jealousy or envy but in searching my heart, I decided those weren't my particular struggles in the moment. More recently, I have unfairly compared myself to other moms who live entirely

Desire fulfilled is sweet to the taste, but fools hate to turn from evil.
Proverbs 13:19

Fools mock at making restitution, but there is goodwill among the upright.
Proverbs 14:9

A wise man is cautious and turns from evil, but a fool is easily angered and is careless.
Proverbs 14:16

different lives, authors who write in completely different ways, or women who have their own unique set of gifts and callings. Every time I found myself in this web of comparison, I'd end up whiney, ungrateful, and eventually without vision.

I could go on confessing my sin to you, but I think you're getting the picture. The idea is that we need to consider more than the "biggies."

"Since we also have such a large cloud of witnesses surrounding us, let us lay aside every weight and the sin that so easily ensnares us, and run with endurance the race that lies before us" (Heb. 12:1.)

Is there a subtle, but powerful sin that has become a hindrance in your pursuit of God? Write a prayer in the margin, asking God to help you lay that sin aside.

3. I've got one final hindrance to mention. Some of us have grown up with a preconceived notion of what a Christian woman is supposed to look like and sound like. Now that we're grown, we've decided we don't want to be like those women. We don't want to dress like them or say the words they say or volunteer for the things they volunteer for. But on the inside we feel the tension. We feel pressure to stick with the mold, stay inside the lines, sound and look just like everybody else. Don't let the mold keep you from God.

What preconceived notions are keeping you from finding your place with God?

_____

" 'Blessed are those who hunger and thirst for righteousness, for they will be filled.' " I hope this week's study has motivated you to do whatever it takes to become a woman who is hungry and thirsty for God. God will do the work that you can't. He will restore what has been lost and renew what you thought was dead. So keep praying until He makes you hungry and thirsty. Persist in prayer until you know that you're falling in love again.

The whole idea of a beautiful offering is that you and I make a conscious choice to lay ourselves on the altar of God. Choice begins with desire and desire comes from hunger. When you and I are starving for God, He calls it beautiful and blessed.

We love a God who is able to multiply whatever we lay on the altar and make it beautiful.

SESSION THREE ❧ VIEWER GUIDE

Who is a God like you,
who pardons sin and forgives the transgression
of the remnant of his inheritance?
You do not stay angry forever
but delight to show mercy (Micah 7:18).

God _____ to show you _____ .

The Spirit of the Sovereign LORD is on me,
*   because the LORD has anointed me to preach good news to the poor.*
He has sent me to bind up the brokenhearted,
*   to proclaim the year of the LORD'S favor and the day of vengeance of our God,*
*   to comfort all who mourn, and provide for those who grieve in Zion—*
*   to bestow on them a crown of beauty instead of ashes,*
*   the oil of gladness instead of mourning,*
*   and a garment of praise instead of a spirit of despair.*
They will be called oaks of righteousness,
*   a planting of the LORD*
*   for the display of his splendor (Isaiah 61:1-3).*

God will take your sack of _____ and replace it with a crown of _____ .

God sent _____ to live and die for the _____ we deserve.

When a woman wears a crown of _____, she knows it came from God's

_____ and _____ .

Blessed are the merciful,
*   for they will be shown mercy (Matthew 5:7).*

A woman who gives out mercy has become a "friend of _____."

God will never ask you to _____ more _____ than He has

already _____ you.

DELIGHTS TO SHOW MERCY

My Father, Today I am specifically praying for *becoming.* Wherever there has been wandering in the life of a woman, bring it to an end so that *becoming* can begin. As You look into the heart of each woman, see her potential. See her fashioned from Your image. See her beauty. Then make her more—more like Your reflection, more like Your plans, more full of Your presence.

Encourage her to dream again, laugh again, feel again. Tenderly whisper Your promise of protection. She belongs to You. No situation can have her. No circumstance can destroy her. No disappointment can overcome her. Reshape our daily lives. Tear down what is misguided. Build strong towers of righteousness. Create women of faith, determined and resilient. Make us merciful. Create pure hearts. Prepare us to stand in strength in the face of persecution. Pour out Your blessings, Lord. Give us kingdom hearts and kingdom lives in the middle of our everyday lives.

For Your glory, in the name of Jesus, Amen.

WEEK THREE ❧

Day 1
When Mercy Steps In

An officer decides not to write a ticket, even though you both know that 78 in a 65 is a violation. After a few words of warning, he lets you drive away. Mercy.

Three weeks overdue, the clerk waives late charges for your DVD rental with a gentle reminder, "Try not to let it happen again." Mercy.

Doctors scratch their heads and say the disease that has been attacking your body has unexplainably gone into remission. Mercy.

He begs for one more chance and something inside you tells you to give it. Mercy.

God says you're forgiven when everyone else treats you like you're not. Mercy.

" 'Blessed are the merciful, because they will be shown mercy.' "
Matthew 5:7

Check the words below that best describe what you think of when you hear *mercy*.

- ❏ kindness
- ❏ charity
- ❏ grace
- ❏ punishment
- ❏ vengeance
- ❏ retribution
- ❏ pity
- ❏ other: _____
- ❏ compassion
- ❏ goodwill
- ❏ generosity

When our God who *is* Mercy comes like a shout into your darkness; when the Father stoops down and tenderly picks up the pieces of your broken life; when Jesus steps in front of what you really deserve; and when the Lord of heaven says, "I still want you," after you thought no one would; mercy is the most amazing truth of all.

Mercy provides a life-giving breath for the one who has been holding her breath. The first good night's sleep in the arms of, "It's going to be okay." A moment of unexpected pardon. A lifetime of clemency. An eternal sigh of relief. Mercy, even in its smallest application, lets you breathe.

Describe a time when you received mercy from God or from another person.

_____

_____

How did receiving that mercy make you feel?

_____

When I receive mercy, several things happen in my heart. I experience an internal struggle connected to not getting what I deserve. I sigh in relief that the punishment or penalty I could have received is dismissed or reduced. I am overwhelmed with gratefulness—tear-producing gratefulness. I develop a real desire for the people I love to experience this same deep breath.

According to Matthew 5:7, what happens to one who shows mercy?

_____

Mercy requires that we:
- *keep short accounts of sin and injustice;*
- *have eyes to see beyond a circumstance and into the heart;*
- *learn to desire the salve of mercy more than the satisfaction of punishment;*
- *be willing to lay down our quick judgment and work on becoming compassionate.*

Speak and act as those who will be judged by the law of freedom. For judgment without mercy will be shown to the one who hasn't shown mercy. Mercy triumphs over judgment.
James 2:12-13

God returns to you the mercy you give away. The one who gives away mercy never runs out of mercy. You cannot outgive the mercy of God.

To effectively give away mercy we must recognize where we have been given mercy; and we must remember the blessing attached to giving mercy away.

We could talk about mercy a hundred ways, but I want us to camp on the intent of Jesus in this verse—giving it away.

The first place I need to give away mercy is perhaps the most trying, my family. I want my children to know what mercy feels like. I want them to grow up and believe they had a merciful mother. I want them to experience the blessings of giving away mercy. But they sometimes make it difficult.

When my children blow it, sometimes because of their blatant, push-mom-over-the-edge disobedience and sometimes because of immaturity or an accident, I get to decide how I will respond. Because of this passage, I decided years ago I wanted mercy to be woven through my parenting. I want our home to operate under the principles Jesus reflected.

Jesus gives people second chances; we will too. Jesus doesn't keep reminding people of their forgiven sin; we'll stop bringing it up. Jesus doesn't always give the full measure of punishment; we'll follow His lead. Jesus let wisdom guide His mercy; so will we.

What other attributes of Jesus' mercy could you model?

_____

What is the biggest hindrance to your giving away mercy at home?

_____

One hindrance might be that no one seems to appreciate your mercy. Another might be the sheer repetition of dealing with these same people in this same house.

Sometimes, when I consider mercy, I realize God is asking me to "die to it." Die to my desire to be right. Die to my desire to have things my way. Die to the unrealistic standards of perfection. Die to my pride. Just die to the arrogance and give mercy.

If God asked you to "die" to an attitude or an action, what would it be?

_____

End today's study by praying about those things to which you need to "die." Ask God to help you lay them at His feet.

DAY 2
BEING MADE PURE

Pure in heart. Every time I write that phrase I feel a sinking feeling in the pit of my stomach. The squeaky whisper from my honest place says, "How?" Not having sex outside marriage sounds like a breeze compared to being pure in heart. This is huge. Holy. All-inclusive. Body, soul, heart, attitude, thought, motive, innuendo, appearance, communication. Pure in heart encompasses every piece of who you are, and having a pure heart makes everything about you pure.

Does that make you want to give up before we even get started? I'm smiling because that happens a lot. That's how we miss opportunities and how we miss maturity. We look at a really big idea and immediately think to ourselves, *I can't.* So we walk away and miss the very thing that could transform our lives.

Being pure in heart is life transforming, mainly because it's so much bigger than we are. It's more about God living in us than God ruling over us. I believe this truth is actually going to give you freedom; hang with me.

> " 'Blessed are the pure in heart,
> because they will see God.' "
> **Matthew 5:8**

> Who can say, "I have kept my heart pure;
> I am cleansed from my sin"?
> **Proverbs 20:9**

Pray and ask God to open your heart. Ask Him to speak into your hidden places. Ask Him to teach you about being pure in heart.

We can do some great things to pursue a more pure life. From the examples listed below, check the area you need to work on and write an action you will take to move toward a more pure life.

❑ strong relationship boundaries
❑ self-discipline regarding my body and mind
❑ accountability
❑ working to break habits that hinder purity
❑ consistent time alone with God
❑ other: _____

Action: _____

_____

All these things are a necessary part of growing in our faith and becoming more like Christ. I can actually work through many of the disciplines during the day and still find myself with impurities. It's one of the frustrating liabilities of our humanity. So what's a woman who wants a pure heart to do? Go to the only One who can make you pure and keep asking.

We will never attain purity and then sustain it for a lifetime. For me, becoming pure in heart is a day-by-day, moment-by-moment cleansing that happens because I humble my grubby heart in the presence of God and beg Him to make it clean again.

Read Psalm 51:1-7 following.

Be gracious to me, God,
according to Your faithful love;
according to Your abundant compassion,
blot out my rebellion.
Wash away my guilt,
and cleanse me from my sin.
For I am conscious of my rebellion,
and my sin is always before me.
Against You—You alone—I have sinned
and done this evil in Your sight.
So You are right when You pass sentence;

You are blameless when You judge.
Indeed, I was guilty [when I] was born;
I was sinful when my mother conceived me.
Surely You desire integrity in the inner self,
and You teach me wisdom deep within.
Purify me with hyssop, and I will be clean;
wash me, and I will be whiter than snow.

To what did King David appeal for righteousness?

_____

Read the rest of Psalm 51 in your Bible. What does David promise God in return for cleansing and strength?

_____

Read Psalm 38:18 and 1 John 1:8-9 in the margin.

What is your responsibility in regard to becoming pure?

_____

What is God's promised response to your confession?

_____

So I confess my guilt;
I am anxious because
* of my sin.*
Psalm 38:18

If we say, "We have no sin," we are deceiving ourselves, and the truth is not in us. If we confess our sins, He is faithful and righteous to forgive us our sins and to cleanse us from all unrighteousness.
1 John 1:8-9

Sometimes I get tired of asking God to make me clean over and over again. He must get tired of me asking. I'm embarrassed that I'm back, unclean in motive or impure in thought. I should be a lot more holy by now. At least it feels like God must think that.

What things make you hesitant to ask God for heart cleansing? Check all that apply and add others that aren't listed.

❑ I'm embarrassed that I have to keep asking.
❑ I'm afraid God will give up on me if I have to keep asking.
❑ I must be really slow to have not caught on yet.
❑ I think He must be too busy with other things to waste time on my same issues over and over again.
❑ Other: _____

I thank God, whom I serve with a clear conscience as my forefathers did, when I constantly remember you in my prayers night and day. … clearly recalling your sincere faith … For this reason I remind you to keep ablaze the gift of God that is in you through the laying on of my hands. For God has not given us a spirit of fearfulness, but one of power, of love and sound judgment.

2 Timothy 1:3,5-7

I have good news! God never tires of our asking. He never minds His beloved running into His arms and begging to look more like Him, less like our humanity.

All I know to do is keep asking God to make me clean. Over the years I have become more personally disciplined. I am more consistent in my study and in my desire. I have accountability. I am learning boundaries. Every place of growth has made a huge difference, but it doesn't keep me constantly pure. Going to God and asking Him to make me pure is the only way.

Second Timothy 1:3,5-7 have profoundly affected me in the past year. Paul is writing to Timothy. That would be Paul the murderer. Paul the hypocrite. Paul the one who doesn't always do what he wants to do. Paul with a clear conscience. Huh?

Paul tells us he is forgiven. He lives the ongoing forgiveness of God. His conscience is clear. Wow! How huge is that? His heart is pure.

From a clear conscience, you can fan into flame the gifts God has put inside you. I hope you are hearing the application for your own life. Do you want to become the woman God dreamed of when He dreamed of you? Do you want to operate in the fullness of your gifts and callings? Do you want to see and do all God has for you? It begins with a clear conscience and a pure heart. Don't be afraid to ask every morning. Don't be timid about receiving forgiveness again. Don't lose heart in staying the course, growing up, laying your impure heart on the altar so it can be made pure one more time.

Would your life be different if you really took God's promise of forgiveness to heart? If so, how?

_____

_____

Do you remember the blessing? The pure in heart get to see God.

Ask God to make your heart pure. Write your prayer in the margin.

Day 3

See the Glory

Some people just have this way about them. They can see God. They can trace His hand of provision. They have a sense about His direction for their lives. They know the right time to pray for a situation and the right time to act. They have great discernment and wisdom. That's the kind of woman I want to become.

Here are my observations about those people who can see God:

- They are spiritually awake and alert.
- They aren't bogged down in sin or wading through mountains of consequences.
- They aren't so mad anymore—either at God or at the way life didn't turn out.
- They are incredibly dependent on being able to see and hear from God.
- They have a holy thirst and aren't satisfied with only a taste of God.
- They have a peaceful glow.
- They walk in the room and see what's right. They can tell you where they believe God is working.

Being able to see the glory of God is the blessing that comes from keeping a pure heart. Let's talk a little about the glory.

Read Exodus 33:18-23 in your Bible. What did Moses ask of God in verse 18?

Why couldn't Moses see all the glory of God?

❑ He would die.
❑ He was distracted.
❑ He had limited capacity.

What part of the glory did God allow Moses to glimpse?

In Ezekiel 3:23, how did the prophet respond to the glory of God?

❏ broke into song   ❏ fell on his face
❏ ran away   ❏ removed his shoes

According to John 1:14 and Hebrews 1:3, how is God's glory manifest in His Son, Jesus?

_____

What is the role of glory in heaven according to Revelation 21:23?

_____

Whenever a person turns to the Lord, the veil is removed. Now the Lord is the Spirit; and where the Spirit of the Lord is, there is freedom. We all, with unveiled faces, are reflecting the glory of the Lord and are being transformed into the same image from glory to glory; this is from the Lord, who is Spirit.
2 Corinthians 3:16-18

Read 2 Corinthians 3:16-18 in the margin. Using the numbers 1-3, put the following statements in the correct order of how we grow to reflect God's glory.

_____ We experience freedom.
_____ We are transformed; we begin to reflect His glory.
_____ The veil is lifted when we turn toward the presence of God.

The woman who can see God begins to reflect His glory as her heart is being made pure and her life is being transformed. That's the woman we are moving toward.

If I asked, "Can you see God?" how would you answer? Check one.

❏ Cannot see, hear, feel, or smell Him. Never have.
❏ Thought I saw Him once a few years ago. A God-encounter.
❏ God-sightings have been sprinkled through the years. Nothing consistent.
❏ I am beginning to see Him more.
❏ I see God all the time. He's everywhere.

When we truly see God, we behold His glory. We begin to see Him working in our lives and beyond our circumstances. We can finally make out the lessons He's been trying to teach us for so long. We glimpse a reason for our suffering. We start to envision our purpose in His amazing plan.

Jesus said that the pure in heart get to see God. Running toward His purity means asking God to do what you can't, praying for change in your attitude, and asking Him to do whatever it takes to clean what has been impure in your life.

These human eyes get to glimpse the glory of His work while we are still on this earth. But one day, when we are with Him in heaven, finally made pure for eternity, then we shall see Him as He is.

Close today's study by reading the words of Job in the margin. Write a prayer asking God to give you a heart that yearns for Him.

_____

_____

*I know that my
Redeemer lives,
and that in the end
he will stand upon
the earth.
And after my skin has
been destroyed,
yet in my flesh I will
see God;
I myself will see him
with my own eyes—
I, and not another.
How my heart yearns
within me!*
Job 19:25-27, NIV

DAY 4
GOD PEACE

I have a girlfriend who has no peace. She is divorced. Three kids. No job. Never finished college. Completely dependent on child support and alimony. She lives in a city without extended family. Both her parents died when she was a teenager. Her house needs repairs she can't afford. She wants a new pair of jeans, a long vacation, and somebody to love her. She feels stress. So she takes it out on her teenage kids and they respond with attitudes that give her more stress. Then she intensifies the pressure and they disconnect even more. She cries. They feel bad and promise to do better. For the past six years she has been caught in the undertow of hopelessness, being pulled out into the sea of despair. She has no peace.

*" 'Blessed are the
peacemakers,
because they will be
called sons of God.' "*
Matthew 5:9

What situations, people, or circumstances seem to steal your peace? Check all that apply and add others as you think of them.

❑ my children
❑ my husband
❑ career demands
❑ taking care of our home

❑ caring for my parents
❑ financial problems
❑ church responsibilities
❑ other: _____

The whole idea of Matthew 5:9 is that you would become a peacemaker. But you can't become a peacemaker until you have become a peace possessor.

We have nothing until we have acquired a personal peace. Think of a woman you know who seems to radiate a heart and countenance of true peace. Write four characteristics that describe her life.

You cannot impart what you do not possess.

_____

_____

Sometimes we don't realize what we're missing until we're beside someone who has it.

Based on the things you just listed and the circumstances in your own life, write four characteristics of peace that you desire for yourself.

_____

_____

Let your gentleness be evident to all. The Lord is near. Do not be anxious about anything, but in everything, by prayer and petition, with thanksgiving, present your requests to God. And the peace of God, which transcends all understanding will guard your hearts and your minds in Christ Jesus.
Philippians 4:5-7, NIV

Look up these passages and answer the following questions about peace.

John 14:27:
Who gives the believer peace?

_____

What should be the result of having a Jesus peace?

❏ never sin again   ❏ hearts unafraid   ❏ boldness to witness

John 16:33:
In a world full of trouble, what hope do we get from this passage?

_____

2 Thessalonians 3:16:
When is peace available to you and me through our Lord Jesus?

_____

Describe a time when you have seen or experienced God's peace.

_____

According to this last passage, peace is available through Jesus at all times and in every circumstance. Do you live like that passage is true?

You want to be a peacemaker, but you don't have peace in your life. You try to get up peaceful everyday and you do okay until somebody speaks to you or one of the kids whacks her brother. You realize instantly that your peace is gone and probably the whole day is going to be without peace.

Jesus has peace. He is the only source of real peace. He is ready and willing to pour out His peace to you. To become a woman of peace, you have to drag your dehydrated heart into the presence of God and ask Him for His peace.

Stay there, in His presence, through prayer or journaling or reading or singing until your heart is peaceful. Jesus has given you peace. He has made you a peace-possessor.

The peace-possessor can become a peacemaker because she has something to give. The peacemaker knows where the peace comes from. She remembers that she cannot become peaceful on her own.

The woman who has become a peacemaker has been given a blessing. She acts like she belongs to the family of God. People see her life and think to themselves, _I wish I could have peace like that. I wonder where her peace comes from._ God-peace stands out.

I love Philippians 4:5-7. Read both translations in the side margins.

I love that _The Message_ paraphrases _peace_ as "a sense of God's wholeness, everything coming together for good." When you and I are in the presence of God, asking for peace, we're asking for an assurance that everything is coming together. God promises to give that. Our assurance that everything is coming together only comes through Jesus. How peace comes into the heart of a troubled woman is a divine mystery, a holy impartation, transcending all understanding.

So take a load off. Rest a little. Take a deep breath and feel yourself push back from the stress. Right in the middle of stupid people and crummy circumstances; even if the mountains of your dreams crumble and wash away to the sea; even through trouble and heartache and disappointment; you can have peace. A Jesus-peace. An I-don't-know-how-but-I-do-know-Who kind of peace.

You belong to God. He wants you to look like the family, to be called His daughter. He'll give you all you need to become a peacemaker.

Make it as clear as you can to all you meet that you're on their side, working with them and not against them. Help them see that the Master is about to arrive. He could show up any minute! Don't fret or worry. Instead of worrying, pray. Let petitions and praises shape your worries into prayers, letting God know of your concerns. Before you know it, a sense of God's wholeness, everything coming together for good, will come and settle you down. It's wonderful what happens when Christ displaces worry at the center of your life.
Philippians 4:5-7,
The Message

DAY 5

A HEART PREPARED

I'm sure you didn't wake up this morning saying to yourself, *I hope today's study is about persecution.* I always want to avoid this one, but we are at the last of the beatitudes and these powerful words are unavoidable. Some weird logic inside us says something like, *If we spend a day studying persecution, then that means it's coming. So maybe we shouldn't talk about it.* But we have to push past our fear and twisted thinking to remember that Scripture exhorts us in 2 Timothy 4:2: "Be prepared in season and out of season; correct, rebuke and encourage—with great patience and careful instruction."

Our spiritual goal for today is preparation.
- If God has begun a life-transforming work in you,
- If you have begun to desire more of Him,
- If you have made a physical and emotional turn in His direction,
- If these truths have begun to impact the way you carry on your everyday life,

then, unfortunately, persecution is probably not far away. I hate telling you that because it sounds discouraging, but hang with me long enough to get to the blessings.

I began to work out about a year ago. I changed my diet, began taking vitamins, lifted weights—the total body makeover kind of change. I found myself wanting a nap for about 10 years and eventually realized another nap wasn't going to help. I needed a stronger body. But some people don't really want you to be stronger and feel better. They roll their eyes and make fun of your commitment. It's mostly innuendo, but you feel it.

In the same way, some people aren't going to be enthusiastic about your life changing or improving. They will sense your increased strength or determination and take a little jab at your resolve. Throw cold water on your passion. Sneak in some emotional sabotage here and there. It may not become a full out assault.

Genesis 50:20 says, "You intended to harm me, but God intended it for good to accomplish what is now being done."

As you grow, improve, and become, some people may be discouraging or even persecuting. How can you prepare yourself now for such a situation?

_____

_____

Satan is all about undermining your life and plans, especially when they involve the glory of God. The people who work with me in ministry have been able to see a very clear pattern of His handiwork over the past years. Whenever I have an important time of ministry or writing in front of me, Satan launches an all out attack of persecution. These very consistent assaults used to break me into pieces.

Satan orchestrates events, circumstances, and even people very close to you to harass you and embarrass you, hoping for your eventual failure. I have always been a cowardly girl. Conflict-avoider. Easygoing, just for the sake of keeping the boat afloat and sailing. But God is making me brave. He has taken me through many episodes of persecution. I have been studying the truth and promises of God in regard to the persecuted. And I have been taking Him at His word. I want the same for you. I want you prepared and strong.

Look back at the Matthew verses in the margin. What are the promises of Jesus for the persecuted?

_____

Earlier in our study we talked about the promise of the kingdom of heaven. What does the kingdom of heaven mean to you?

_____

_____

We'll talk more about rewards in heaven. But for now, what kind of rewards do you believe heaven holds?

_____

_____

What is God's instruction in Psalm 37:1-6 regarding evil men?

_____

" 'Blessed are those who are persecuted for righteousness, because the kingdom of heaven is theirs.' "
Matthew 5:10

" 'Blessed are you when they insult you and persecute you and falsely say every kind of evil against you because of Me. Be glad and rejoice, because your reward is great in heaven.' "
Matthew 5:11-12

Why? _____

From verses 3-6 (NIV), fill in the blanks about God's instructions to us:

_____ in the Lord and do good.

_____ in the land and _____ safe pasture.

_____ yourself in the Lord and he will give you the

_____ of your heart.

_____ your way to the Lord;

_____ in him and he will do this:

He will make your _____ shine like the dawn, the justice of your cause like the noonday sun.

In times of persecution and heartache, our responsibility is to stay focused on the call. Eyes squarely fixed on the goal. Trusting God to hold us in what can feel like a free fall. Expecting God to honor righteousness over evil.

Read 1 Peter 3:13-15 in the margin. Underline the directives Peter gives to us regarding suffering and persecution.

You cannot give an answer to anyone regarding your hope, unless the answer has come to abide in your heart.

Spend a few moments reading back through your study today. Pray and ask God to prepare your heart and mind. Ask Him to help you recall His promises. Ask Him to give you a holy confidence, even in the middle of attacks. Ask Him to make you ready, in season and out.

Who will harm you if you are passionate for what is good? But even if you should suffer for righteousness, you are blessed. Do not fear what they fear or be disturbed, but set apart the Messiah as Lord in your hearts, and always be ready to give a defense to anyone who asks you for a reason for the hope that is in you.
1 Peter 3:13-15

SESSION FOUR ✤ VIEWER GUIDE

God's standards call you to a life of _____.

When you fail, God promises to catch you in His net of _____.

When God calls you to obedience, _____ Him because

He is _____ about you.

" 'You are the salt of the earth. But if the salt loses its saltiness, how can it be made salty again? It is no longer good for anything, except to be thrown out and trampled by men' " **(Matthew 5:13).**

God can use the _____ woman with her

_____ life.

" 'You are the light of the world. A city on a hill cannot be hidden. Neither do people light a lamp and put it under a bowl. Instead they put it on its stand, and it gives light to everyone in the house. In the same way, let your light shine before men, that they may see your good deeds and praise your Father in heaven' " **(Matthew 5:14-16).**

The grown-up woman has a bright _____ for Jesus.

YOU BELONG TO HEAVEN

Oh Father, Take this truth and burn it deeply into the soul—You use ordinary for Your glory. Give each woman a great assurance of Your delight, even when she feels ordinary and plain. She is Your beloved. Your favor rests on her. Help her understand this truth in a fresh way. May it give her courage, peace, and strength.

You make extraordinary things happen from ordinary lives. Help us submit our lives for Your purpose. Show us how to bend our hearts in Your presence. Cover every weakness that keeps us from growing and becoming. God, I want You in every corner of my common. Take over the whole thing. Make it obvious at every turn. You can fill a common woman with Your uncommon glory. You will use anybody who lays her life at Your feet.

Where we have been dim or even dark, turn on every light of Your radiance. Where we have hidden or been hesitant, teach us to run into the wide-open space of Your love. May Your light inside us begin to shine. May others see You because we do not keep You hidden.

By Your grace, we can shine. In the name of Jesus, Amen.

WEEK FOUR ❧

Day 1

As You Go

Over the past three weeks we've been studying the first section of the Sermon on the Mount. We called those blessings the "When You Are's." When you lay your life on the altar of God, even though imperfect, the covering of Jesus makes it beautiful. The decision to make your life an offering is the first step toward becoming the woman God has envisioned in you.

In the rest of Jesus' amazing sermon, He's going to give us rich instruction for "As You Go." We don't have time in this study to dive into each element of the teaching, but I hope you get enough to make you want more. I think when these words begin to intersect our everyday lives, we will begin to experience a power and passion we haven't known before. When we begin to orchestrate everyday around Jesus' call, I believe we'll begin to have eyes to see, ears to hear, and hearts that desire to respond.

Let your guard down a bit. Be ready to embrace the call to obedience. Anticipate that God might want to rearrange your whole life around His plans. Try not to shrink back if the Holy Spirit prompts you to reconsider your relationship patterns or your emotional health or your spiritual life with Him. Give Him permission to permeate every area of your heart.

Are there areas of your heart still shut down to God? Write a prayer inviting Him into every hidden place.

_____

_____

How willing are you to wholeheartedly follow Christ, no matter where He leads? Place an X on the continuum to indicate where you are right now.

I'm still a little scared.	My head wants to trust, but my heart isn't there yet.	I'm ready. Let's go!

This sermon is crammed with ideas and principles that really impact our lives. Most of these lessons involve a greater trust. Trusting the words of Jesus, the heart of the Father, His ability to speak so we can hear.

Sometimes when I am learning to trust God more, it feels like a free fall. I am giving up control. Letting go and trusting feels like falling, because I've been trying so desperately to hang on, navigate my circumstances, anticipate the unknown, and find order in the chaos.

For me, trusting is learning to breathe during the fall. Trusting is believing with my whole life that God will catch me. He promises to keep His promises. He is able. He is strong. His heart toward me is good. He wants even more for me than I can dream. He is bigger than all of us.

Becoming more like Jesus and trying on these truths, as you go, will involve new levels of trust. As you sort through your trust issues and your commitment to trust, it might help to begin small. Choose one particular idea, person, event, or circumstance that seems to consume your life right now. With that one thing in mind, walk through the next steps with me.

1. Name the circumstance you want to entrust to God. Write in

    code if you need to. _____

2. Pray this passage from your heart. Insert your name and your circumstance where appropriate.
   I know whom I have believed, and am convinced that he is able to guard what I have entrusted to him for that day (2 Tim. 1:12, NIV).

3. Be quiet for a few moments. Close your eyes and picture yourself being caught and held in the strong arms of Jesus. Describe how it feels to see yourself inside God's embrace.

    _____

    _____

4. Pray through this passage in the same way.
   No eye has see,
     no ear has heard,
   no mind has conceived
     what God has prepared for those who love him (1 Cor. 2:9, NIV).

Trusting means living like this verse is true. I cannot see. I cannot hear. I cannot conceive. But I trust that the God who loves me has prepared more than I can imagine.

If we begin with a small step of trust, then God rushes in to prove He is faithful. When we have seen His faithfulness, we learn to trust more and respond quickly to His prompting.

In these next weeks, we'll focus on what a woman of God looks like—spiritually clean, tenderhearted, ready to hear God's voice, eager to grow, ready to trust. It's time to let God begin shaping His dream woman. It's time for each one of us to live like we belong to the kingdom of heaven.

Continue with your prayer time. Read aloud the truths listed below and ask God to help you begin afresh with this resolve.

God is wildly in love with me.
He sent His Son to die for me.
He always comes for me.
He never leaves me.
He always hears my whispered prayers.
I am going to trust that His promises are true.
I am going to trust that His words are perfect.
I am going to trust Him beyond my understanding.
I am going to lay my life before Him.
By His grace, I am going to become the woman He dreamed of.

This kind of determination may make you feel anxious. You may feel like I'm setting you up to fail again. Unfortunately, we are all probably going to blow it again. Our humanity is frustrating. Tomorrow we're going to talk about the grace God provides for the women who decide to go for it. His net of grace grabs us, puts us back on our feet, and lets us keep running forward.

Stay strong, dear one. God is so faithful. Lean into Him. Put the full weight of your life onto His broad shoulders. He makes all things possible.

> *Many are the woes of the wicked, but the Lord's unfailing love surrounds the man who trusts in him.*
> **Psalm 32:10, NIV**

> *For the LORD God is a sun and shield.*
> *the LORD gives grace and glory;*
> *He does not withhold the good*
> *from those who live with integrity.*
> **Psalm 84:11**

DAY 2

GRACE AS YOU GO

If we only get to go forward in life because we deserve to, then I'm sunk. If we only take the next step of maturity because of right choices or perfect attendance, then most of us will remain babies. If only the flawless can use their gifts, then no one can.

God has paved the way for us by the beautiful gift of His grace. We enter through grace, walk with the strength God gives by grace, and keep going only because grace picks us up and nudges us along.

The woman who loves God gets to become more than anyone imagined because grace can cover every weakness.

Read the following passages and match each reference to what it tells us about God's grace.

Isaiah 61:1   God's grace is sufficient.

1 Corinthians 1:27-30   The Holy Spirit empowers us
                                        to show grace to others.

2 Corinthians 12:9   God chose us for His grace.

Write your definition of *grace*.

_____

_____

God's grace for my life means that ...

_____

_____

It's never too late to become the women He wants us to be. Because of grace, we haven't gone too far or spent too much or stayed too long.

God provided us grace for salvation through Jesus' death on the cross. It is a means by which the ungodly or undeserving person (like you and me) can have a relationship with God.

As you read the passages below, circle the words that describe our spiritual condition before we knew Christ.

While we were still helpless, at the appointed moment, Christ died for the ungodly. For rarely will someone die for a just person—though for a good person perhaps someone might even dare to die. But God proves His own love for us in that while we were still sinners Christ died for us! (Rom. 5:6-8).

God, who is abundant in mercy, because of His great love that He had for us, made us alive with the Messiah even though we were dead in trespasses. By grace you are saved! (Eph. 2:4-5).

Now go back and underline the words that tell how Christ made a way for us. Put a big box around the reason God has given us grace through Jesus.

Read Ephesians 2:6-9 in the margin and answer the questions.

Because of grace, where is our new place, our new seat?

_____

According to this passage, what have you done to deserve the grace of God?

_____

What about the person sitting next to you. What has she done to deserve the grace of God?

_____

He also raised us up with Him and seated us with Him in the heavens, in Christ Jesus, so that in the coming ages He might display the immeasurable riches of His grace in His kindness to us in Christ Jesus. For by grace you are saved through faith, and this is not from yourselves; it is God's gift—not from works, so that no one can boast.
Ephesians 2:6-9

"Since we have been justified through faith, we have peace with God through our Lord Jesus Christ, through whom we have gained access by faith into *this grace in which we now stand*" (Rom. 5:1-2, NIV, emphasis mine).

Stay with me, because this is important. When we call Jesus Christ our Savior by faith that means we acknowledge His death has paid the penalty for our sin. Our faith in Jesus makes us "justified" before God. That same faith also gives us peace with God.

Remember the old definition that helps us understand justified: "just as if I'd never sinned."

His grace is more than that one-time saving event. We now stand in His grace. His grace gives life, matures us, provides ongoing forgiveness, and allows us to become.

God gifts us to live out our days inside the blessing of His grace. I hope these passages have the same affect on your heart they have on mine. These truths remind me how great the love of God truly is. How freely He has given eternal life to me. How sweet that He gives grace for me to stand in everyday. And they remind me how little I have to do with any of it.

My heart feels so grateful. Because of His grace to me, my spirit is renewed. I want to return God's lavish love with the offering of my life.

> *"'You are the salt of the earth. But if the salt should lose its taste, how can it be made salty? It's no longer good for anything but to be thrown out and trampled on by men.' "*
> **Matthew 5:13**

> *"'Let me tell you why you are here. You're here to be salt-seasoning that brings out the God-flavors of this earth. If you lose your saltiness, how will people taste godliness? You've lost your usefulness and will end up in the garbage.' "*
> **Matthew 5:13,**
> ***The Message***

> *"'Go, therefore, and make disciples of all nations, baptizing them in the name of the Father and of the Son and of the Holy Spirit, teaching them to observe everything I have commanded you. And remember, I am with you always, to the end of the age.' "*
> **Matthew 28:19-20**

I want to walk in obedience. I want to put on His precepts and imitate His character. By His grace I am able and so are you.

As you finish this day of study. Spend some time sharing your grateful heart with God in prayer.

DAY 3
COMMON SALT

In Matthew 5:13, Jesus proclaims with authority that the ones who follow Him are called to be the salt of the earth. Salt preserves and purifies but not inside the shaker. It only works after it has been rubbed into the food.

In the same way, to be effective you and I must be rubbed into a dying world, interacting, loving, and becoming right along with them. It's a little scary, especially if we have become the church ladies who live inside the church bubble. Personally, I have to make a conscious effort to be rubbed into the world and meet people outside my Jesus circle.

Sometimes we find ourselves in places that need salt, but we don't allow ourselves to be rubbed in. We can go to the gym or the salon with the rest of the world but never interact or build relationships.

Write down three places you have an opportunity to be salt.

_____

Now write the names or initials of three people God has sent into your life who need the saltiness of Jesus sprinkled generously over them. (I promise He has sent them, even if you missed them!)

_____

Matthew 28:19-20 is called the Great Commission. Jesus instructs His followers to go. Go get yourselves rubbed into the lives of others so they will be able to taste the presence of God.

In Acts 1:8 Jesus instructs the disciples to begin in Jerusalem. That's where they were at the time, their home. If you aren't sure where your saltiness is supposed to begin, start in your Jerusalem, your home. Begin with the people you live with or around.

Then Jesus told them to go into Judea and Samaria. That was the next circle out for them, their north and south. This circle includes neighbors, business relationships, and people we have the opportunity to meet.

And, finally, Jesus said to go to the ends of the earth. The ends of the earth for me is people outside my normal, everyday life. People I make an effort to get to know because they matter to God. Sometimes I'm in this circle trying to rub in salt when I'm at the rescue mission talking to strangers who live incredibly different and sometimes dangerous lives. Sometimes I'm literally at the ends of the earth in a foreign country. I am trying to leave myself open to God's prompting about where and when I am supposed to get out of everything I find familiar and go.

Stop now and ask the Lord to help you develop a plan during this week of study for how you can be His witness in Jerusalem, Judea, and the ends of the earth. As these plans come together, write them on the lines below.

My Jerusalem_____

_____

My Judea _____

_____

The ends of my earth _____

_____

" 'You will receive power when the Holy Spirit has come upon you, and you will be My witnesses in Jerusalem, in all Judea and Samaria, and to the ends of the earth.' "
Acts 1:8

Salt provides flavor. You can find yourself exactly where you are supposed to be, right place, right time, right people, and yet never give them anything that brings out the "God-flavor." We usually keep quiet for a couple of reasons: We either (1) think we have nothing to say, or (2) we're afraid.

So here's my best advice. You want to be salt? You want to flavor the world with God's ideas, His love, and His compassion? Practice.

Practice your God-flavoring with people who aren't threatening. Your kids. Your neighbor's preschooler. Your dog. When you are becoming God-flavor, you are pointing other people to God. Some of you may be afraid you'll say the wrong thing, but I promise if you jump in God will take over.

I was on a long flight recently and had an extended conversation with the guy sitting next to me. At one point he told me he was very successful in his business and that he'd been lucky. Without thinking, even without hesitation, these words came out of my mouth, "The Bible says every good gift comes to us from God. If your business is good, it came directly to you from the hand of God. No luck about it. You have been blessed."

I stopped myself just before I was going to quote the chapter and verse. *Just a little salt at a time, Angela. You don't want this man to choke.* But God was doing what God does and the man said to me, "You know I haven't ever thought about it like that. I have been blessed. All those things have come to me from God."

Salt brings out the God-flavor. Salt makes you thirsty. Do you make anyone thirsty for Jesus? Do you remind others of His presence, His work among us, and His calling toward Christlikeness? Do others see the person of God because they shared a life experience with you?

Lots of people know what Christians are against. But do they know what we're for? Do they know that we are for their healing and their becoming strong? Do they know we want them to have victory instead of defeat? Do they know we have compassion for their weakness? Do they know about our forgiveness?

I think if they knew it would make them thirsty.

Make a list of eight attributes of Christ that you want people to learn through their relationship with you.

_____   _____

_____   _____

_____   _____

_____   _____

Salt is a common substance. Feeling kind of plain today? Then you're the kind of woman God's looking for.

I am sitting on my bed, typing on my laptop. I have on gym shorts and a t-shirt. My three-day hair is in a ponytail, kind of. I'm wearing no makeup because my face is doing that mid-life breakout thing. My legs have gross bruises and varicose veins. The dryer is buzzing. There are piles of folded laundry on the other side of my bed that need to be put away. I just went down the hall to reprimand the boys for fighting over a pencil— like we only have one. My life is so very common, and yet, God can use a woman like me.

What things make your life feel common?

_____

How do these things affect how God can use you?

_____

How cool to know that God wants to use a common woman like you too!

DAY 4
LIGHT THROUGH YOUR ORDINARY

A few weeks ago I returned from a trip to South Africa. Before I left, one of the organizers came to me and said through her beautiful English accent, "Angela, I hope you won't be offended by what I'm going to say to you."

I braced myself for something critical.

"Angela, I have decided why we all love you. It's because you're so very ordinary. We feel like you're just one of us, but Jesus shines through you."

I gave her the biggest hug. I don't think she could have given me a compliment I'd have liked any more.

Yesterday we talked about being common like salt. Yet, even in our common lives, Jesus is entrusting us with the amazing message of His love to take to the ends of the earth. Maybe you feel ordinary. Maybe you aren't sure that the light of the world could ever shine through a woman like you. What if being ordinary is the whole point? I think Jesus knows exactly what He is asking when He calls ordinary women, broken women, or less than perfect women to be the light of the world.

Read John 8:12 in the margin. What does Jesus call Himself?

_____

How do you and I become "light"?_____

To shine like the light of the world means to reflect to everyone around you what God has done for you (see 1 Peter 2:9-10).

Have you been forgiven? Then shine forgiveness.

" 'No one lights a lamp and puts it under a basket, but rather on a lampstand, and it gives light for all who are in the house. In the same way, let your light shine before men, so that they may see your good works and give glory to your Father in heaven.' "
Matthew 5:15-16

" 'I am the light of the world. Anyone who follows Me will never walk in the darkness but will have the light of life.' "
John 8:12

Have you been set free? Then radiate freedom to others.
Have you been rescued? Then show others your rescuing God.
Have you been given grace? Then spread grace all around you.
Have you been given eternity? Then illuminate the Way.

Read the paraphrase of Matthew 5:15-16 below and underline the phrases that suggest actions we are to take.

Here's another way to put it: You're here to be light, bringing out the God-colors in the world. God is not a secret to be kept. We're going public with this, as public as a city on a hill. If I make you light-bearers, you don't think I'm going to hide you under a bucket, do you? I'm putting you on a light stand. Now that I've put you there on a light stand—shine! Keep open house; be generous with your lives. By opening up to others, you'll prompt people to open up with God, this generous Father in heaven (Matt. 5:15-16, *The Message*).

If you practice this passage, you won't say, "My faith is a private thing." Some things in your life may be personal and private. I have those as well, but I cannot keep inside the powerful effect God's love has made in my life. This kind of faith changes a woman's countenance. She walks into the room glowing, even in her ordinary. It changes the way we love and receive love.

If you went public with your light, if you became as bright as a "city on a hill," how would that change your normal experience?

_____

_____

I believe when a woman who belongs to Jesus walks into the room, the glory of God should walk in with her. I believe our lives should be such a grateful reflection that it can't be contained. Enough 20-watt-bulb living. Enough private, we-don't-talk-about-our-faith whispering. It's time to be the city and shine! Shine through your ordinary. Shine through your broken places. Just shine!

Does this shining thing ❏ feel scary or does it ❏ inspire you? (Check one.) Why?

_____

_____

The LORD is my light and my salvation— whom shall I fear?
Psalm 27:1

If it feels scary, what holds you back?

_____

Spend some time in prayer giving any hesitancy or fears to God.

A brilliant light is the result of a deeper walk with Jesus. We cannot fake light for Christ, although many, including me, have tried. We will not shine like a city on a hill without a close fellowship with God.

I think the coolest thing about becoming the light of the world is that we get to introduce people to the Father of Lights. We have the privilege of carrying His light into their darkness. Hopeless people get a second chance, and the light of Christ introduces the lost to a brand new way.

Ministry for me began with the youth group at my church. Every time a kid began to understand the unconditional love of God, a light came on in his or her life. As I watched those kids, one by one, become brighter and brighter, I was hooked. Ridiculously addicted to Light transformation. Sold out. I made a lifetime commitment to shining. When you begin to see what the light of Christ can do through an ordinary you, I trust you'll be well on your way to being ridiculously addicted too.

Before we wrap up today, I want to look at another phrase from Matthew 5:15-16 in _The Message_. "Be generous with your lives." I love that. To shine like a city on a hill is to be generous with our lives. Generous with our homes, our affection, our stuff, our attention, our forgiveness. Living with open arms. Interruptible. Patient. Interested. Passionate.

What are three actions you can take this week to be more generous with your life?

1. _____

2. _____

3. _____

It's time to go be the light of the world. Don't hide what Christ is doing in your life. Let the people around you see your Father in heaven.

Sometimes it takes courage to shine. Ask God.

Sometimes it takes a commitment. Ask God.

But sometimes, all a woman has to do is show up and put her lamp on a stand. Go get 'em.

BE RECONCILED

> " 'If you are offering your gift at the altar, and there remember that your brother has something against you, leave your gift there in front of the altar. First go and be reconciled to your brother, then come and offer your gift.' "
>
> **Matthew 5:23-24**

If you have made it this far in the study, I assume it's because you truly want to return God's love with your life. I hope you are hearing the Father speak His unconditional love for you. Move in closer and feel the tenderness of His affection. Understand the goodness of His heart. Experience His unrelenting pursuit of your heart.

Jesus also calls us to obedience. That's why today's verses can sometimes be difficult.

A friend just dropped by and asked which study I'm writing. I told her. She laughingly said, "I always skip over those verses." Obedience is the path that moves us closer to our Father; and sometimes the obedience Jesus teaches takes us right into the middle of the verses we hoped to skip.

Reconciliation requires humility. And maturity. And discipline. And courage. I'm sure you know a lot of people, just like I do, who've been severely wounded in relationships. It's one thing to observe conflict in others; it's a gross, ugly deal to admit that the one who is not reconciled is you. Wrongs you've committed. Forgiveness you've denied. Grudges you hold. Vengeance you desire. Anger you feed. On and on.

Every time I get an idea that seems bigger than me—you know, a Jesus instruction that makes my stomach hurt—I immediately know that obedience is going to require surrender. I'm probably going to have to give something up. Eventually I may need to die to it. I imagine obedience is sometimes the same for you.

What attitudes or behaviors would you have to give up to make room for obedience? Check all that apply.

❑ selfishness   ❑ fear   ❑ pride
❑ desire for revenge   ❑ doubt   ❑ control
❑ need to be right   ❑ other: _____

Circle the one that is most difficult for you to surrender.

As our lives are becoming beautiful offerings, it's time to remember if there is anyone who has something against us. As we consider these people, the first step is to acknowledge our sin to ourselves and to God. It's our responsibility to own the part we play in the disagreement, misunderstanding, or conflict. Second, it's our responsibility to move toward that person. In this passage, the specifics are clear. We are to go toward the one who is offended, hurt, or misunderstood.

Fill in the chart below. Write the name, initials, or code word for person(s) who have something against you. Next write your part of the responsibility. Finally, write what the Lord is calling you to surrender in each relationship. Refer to the list of attitudes and behaviors in the previous activity.

Relationship	My responsibility	What I'm called to surrender

" 'Reach a settlement quickly with your adversary.' "
Matthew 5:25

Make every effort to live in peace with all men and to be holy.
Hebrews 12:14

Now for the double-whammy. Go immediately and work toward making things right.

Sometimes I wish Jesus had said, "Take your time with this kind of thing. I realize the whole idea is humbling and it could take years to work up your courage." But He didn't. He is walking us down a path of maturity. Pursuing this kind of character forces us to grow up.

This may open up a huge can of worms for you. Some things cannot be resolved overnight or in one conversation. One heartfelt apology might not get it. You may need to seek wise counsel from your church leaders, a godly counselor, or a friend who understands your heart. This could take a while, but the most important part is that you begin immediately. Christians are called to settle matters quickly (see Matt. 5:25).

What does "make every effort" mean? (see Hebrews 12:14)

❑ Pray. Ask God for forgiveness. Receive His forgiveness. Get on with life.

❑ Pray about it one time. Send an e-mail. Never bring it up again. You tried.

❑ Pray. Surrender anything that keeps you paralyzed. Go, even with butterflies in the pit of your stomach. Ask for reconciliation. Make every effort until the person knows that your heart is good and your desire is peace.

The answer should be obvious, but what if I asked you how you have *lived out* the concept of "make every effort"? Would your answer be different? If so, circle how you would respond.

Maybe you've been stingy with your forgiveness. Sometimes we just don't feel like forgiving and doing the hard work of repair. I cannot give more forgiveness than God has already given me. He would never ask me to reconcile if He had not already made a way. Read 2 Corinthians 5:18-21 in the margin.

How does God reconcile Himself to the world?

_____

What does reconcile mean according to verse 19?

_____

How would that apply to our earthly relationships?

_____

We are therefore Christ's what?_____

18Everything is from God, who reconciled us to Himself through Christ and gave us the ministry of reconciliation: 19that is, in Christ, God was reconciling the world to Himself, not counting their trespasses against them, and He has committed the message of reconciliation to us. 20Therefore, we are ambassadors for Christ, certain that God is appealing through us, we plead on Christ's behalf, "Be reconciled to God." 21He made the One who did not know sin to be sin for us, so that we might become the righteousness of God in Him.

2 Corinthians 5:18-21

Because we follow the teachings of Jesus, in this case making every effort to reconcile ourselves in broken relationships, others can see we represent a God who does the same. He reconciles Himself to sinful men and women. He doesn't count their sin against them. If we are going to be like Him, obedience requires that we work to live at peace.

It's messy and it requires emotion, but surrendering to the process of reconciliation may be one of the most important things you'll ever do for your character.

This may have been a difficult day of study for you. Spend some time in prayer with the Father. Affirm to Him your desire to live a beautiful life. Tell Him you want to live this passage. Ask for courage even in the hard places. Write your prayer in the margin.

I promise He'll walk you through.

SESSION FIVE ❧ VIEWER GUIDE

Matthew 6:1-6

Matthew 6:16-18

In the _____ place, God comes to _____ your soul.

2 Timothy 3:6-7

If you are having a _____ life with God, there should be _____ in your life.

To develop a secret life with God, you must be _____.

      P _____
      R _____
      A _____
      Y _____

When you give, pray, and fast in secret, God adds _____ to your everyday life.

2 Timothy 1:3

In the secret place, God will give you a clear _____.

When God makes you _____, it doesn't matter what comes against you.

Matthew 6:19-21

In the secret place, you begin to store up _____ in heaven.

Matthew 6:25

If you give yourself to _____, it will keep you from the secret life.

Matthew 6:33

When it feels like you're _____, go to your secret place.

When it feels like all hell is coming against you, break _____ loose in your secret place.

KEEPING A SECRET LIFE

Father, Teach us to foster our faith in the
unseen. Give us a yearning for a secret life
with You and an expectation that You
will show up in our darkness.

Please give spiritual anticipation—a desire
to know what our lives could look like if
we nourish a deeper, private walk with You.
God, give us specifics—the where and when
and how of this secret journey. Teach and
challenge us in these next days. We want to
know You in private and hear You in whispers.
For every step my sister takes, bless her
with encouragement and more desire. Meet
with her in the prayer closet and assure her of
Your presence and pleasure. Give clear guidance
and soul peace. Restore the abiding joy that comes
from assurance.
Father, cover this week in Your mercy. Hold back
discouragement and failure. Come everyday with a fresh
outpouring of Your love. Speak into our loneliness. Strengthen
our weakness. Stand us up and send us out refilled by Your glory.

In the precious name of Jesus, Amen.

WEEK FIVE ❧

DAY 1
GIVING IN SECRET

" 'Be careful not to practice your righteousness in front of people, to be seen by them' " (Matt. 6:1). I love that God wants a secret relationship with me. I crave intimacy, and the Father's personal attention is just about as intimate as it gets.

Only the Father sees three beautiful pieces of our lives. Three acts of service, offered in private, get the attention of God. Giving in secret. Praying in secret. Fasting in secret. God holds these attributes in such high esteem that He promises to reward our lives when we're keeping the secrets.

Maybe this excites me because most of my God-life is so public. Nothing makes me happier than talking to people about Jesus. Everything inside me was made for this. But I don't have anything to give without my secret life with God.

> " 'When you give to the poor, don't let you left hand know what your right hand is doing, so that your giving may be in secret. And your Father who sees in secret will reward you.' "
> **Matthew 6:3-4**

Read 2 Corinthians 8:7; 9:6-7,10-11 from your Bible and answer the following questions.

What is Paul's final exhortation in 2 Corinthians 8:7?

_____

According to 2 Corinthians 9:6-7, what is the promised blessing when we sow (or give) generously? _____

What is the giving attitude that God loves? _____

According to 2 Corinthians 9:10-11, who will supply all that you need to be generous? _____

What happens because of your generosity?

_____

Giving reminds me of a phrase we talked about a few days ago, "Be generous with your lives" (week 4, day 4). The application is also appropriate here. Be generous when you give in secret.

If there is a poor person among you, one of your brothers within any of your gates in the land the LORD your God is giving you, you must not be hardhearted or tightfisted toward your poor brother. Instead, you are to open your hand to him and freely loan him enough for whatever need he has. Be careful that there isn't this wicked thought in your heart, 'The seventh year, the year of canceling debts, is near,' and you are stingy toward your poor brother and give him nothing. He will cry out to the LORD against you, and you will be guilty. Give to him, and don't have a stingy heart when you give, and because of this the LORD your God will bless you in all your work and in everything you do.
Deuteronomy 15:7-10

Read Deuteronomy 15:7-10 in the margin. Matthew 6:3-4 says there will be a reward for our secret giving. Underline the reward that is promised in Deuteronomy 15:10.

As you and I grow in the discipline of quiet giving, God has promised to reward. A part of His reward includes an extra provision of His resources, energy, and joy. As we give, God provides more to give. He increases our desire to give. And He multiplies the joy we come to know in this secret discipline by His joy over us.

As secret giving becomes part of our character, a few things begin to happen. The woman God transforms into His likeness gives so readily and easily that she hardly reflects on what she is doing. She barely notices her own good deeds and rarely remembers them. Giving becomes "no big deal" for the one who learns to give in secret and without regard for attention or approval. As this transformation takes place, we need to remember to ask God several things.

Ask God for eyes to see. Needs surround us, but sometimes we miss them. As a part of your prayer time, ask God for eyes to see where He is calling you to give in secret. Ask Him to make it obvious when He wants you to be the giver.

Ask God for a heart to respond. "If anyone has this world's goods and sees his brother in need but shuts off his compassion from him—how can God's love reside in him? Little children, we must not love in word or speech, but in deed and truth" (1 John 3:17-18). Ask God to help you take action. So many times we miss the blessing because our hearts were prompted by the Holy Spirit and we filed it away for another time.

Ask God for creativity in your giving. Giving money is necessary, and some needs cannot be met otherwise. But it's not the only way to give in secret.

Write down 6 creative ways to give in secret apart from giving money. I've supplied two examples to get you started.

Send dinner to a neighbor   Leave flowers for a friend

_____   _____

_____   _____

_____   _____

This area of your life is so valuable that it requires your determination to develop and protect these disciplines. Every once in a while God speaks to me in the chaos, but more often I hear Him in the quiet, in the secret.

Yesterday was Sunday and my pastor's sermon was great. I heard powerful teaching regarding my life with God. But this morning, in secret, I prayed through my notes and took another look at a few verses. In the quiet, I heard God's application of yesterday's sermon. My pastor is a great teacher, but he is only a messenger. The Holy Spirit is the prompter. He is the One who gives direction to our giving and responding. As we cultivate a secret life, our sensitivity to the guidance of the Holy Spirit will also sharpen and expand.

When we keep a secret life, the applause of God will be deafening. A part of our kingdom living is incredibly public. We're supposed to shine like a city on a hill. But there is a private kingdom life, with undercover elements that become spiritual acts of worship. This viewing is reserved just for Him. No one else sees your performance played out inside God's closed theater. But He does and He cheers for an encore. From your secret giving, you will experience a pleasure that doesn't come any other way and the blessing of God's promised reward for your obedience.

How often should you give in secret? Every time the Holy Spirit says give. How much should you give? Everything He wants you to give. How much will it cost you? It'll probably cost a little time and a little energy and a little money. But have you ever watched God multiply your sacrifice and give it back to you? You'll be amazed to see how God does accounting in the economy of secret giving.

Look back at the creative ways of giving you listed earlier. Put a star beside the idea that most tugs at your heart. Which idea could you respond to immediately?

_____

How? _____

Close in prayer, asking the Lord to provide you opportunities to give in secret.

DAY 2

PRAYING IN SECRET

" 'Whenever you pray, you must not be like the hypocrites, because they love to pray standing in the synagogues and on the street corners to be seen by people. I assure you: They've got their reward! But when you pray, go into your private room, shut your door, and pray to your Father who is in secret. And your Father who sees in secret will reward you.' "
Matthew 6:5-6

Today we are going to spend some time in guided prayer. I am convinced we learn more about praying and become better at it through practice.

Because of our human condition and because of the enemy's work, you may be thinking, *Not today. I don't have time to stop for this.* Maybe something in your spirit just doesn't feel like praying. Every time that happens to me, sirens go off in my head and red warning flags begin waving in my heart. If I don't feel like praying, I have learned that means I really need to pray, and soon. If you have those sirens going off in your head, make a concerted effort to push through your apathy or distraction and lean into this time of prayer.

Find a place you can be alone with God in quiet and secret. Take your Bible and a pen. Begin by reading Matthew 6:5-6.

When I finally get into my closet to pray, it seems like my mind is always racing. Sometimes I'm even out of breath from the pace it took to get here. I always want to begin my prayer time with my heart focused on the glory of God, but sometimes I can't get there immediately. I have to ask for cleansing. I ask Him to settle my heart so I can speak and hear and reflect on Him.

Spend the first part of your prayer time in surrender. I usually lay on my face down here with the shoeboxes. In these surrender prayers I even hold out my hands to show God that I want to put down all the distractions I hauled into the closet. When I am here in secret, only God sees. I don't feel weird or hokey. This is my prayer offering to God and I want even my physical posture to reflect my heart. Do whatever it takes to place yourself in secret before the Lord. This is your special, secret time with God.

Turn in your Bible to Psalm 29 and read it out loud. Now read Psalm 33. There in your closet, pray back to God your praise and your worship for all the attributes you just read. Look back at the words if you need to and specifically thank God as He leads you.

Go back to Psalm 33:20-22.
- Commit anew that you will wait for God in all your requests.
- Affirm that your hope is in Him.
- Ask for His unfailing love to rest upon you.

Turn to Psalm 51:1-12 and read that passage to God.
- Spend time praying through each individual transgression that the Holy Spirit brings to mind.
- Ask for cleansing and purity.
- Ask for strength in future temptation.
- Confess anything that hinders you in your relationship with God.
- Receive God's pardon as a gift. Thank Him.

You may already keep a prayer journal of ongoing requests to God. This is a great way to record God's faithfulness. If not, write your requests below.

_____

_____

Spend a few minutes praying for each request individually. Cover each of these needs with your desire for God's will to be done.

Do not lose heart in your prayers. Remember we just made a commitment to wait on God. In our waiting, we pray until the answer has been given. Ask God for all that you need. You know part of what you need and God knows the rest.

Next pray through the Lord's Prayer:

" 'Our Father in heaven,
  Your name be honored as holy.
  Your kingdom come.
  Your will be done
  on earth as it is in heaven.
  Give us today our daily bread.
  And forgive us our debts,
  as we also have forgiven our debtors.
  And do not bring us into temptation,
  but deliver us from the evil one' " (Matthew 6:9-13).

We have access to God because of the work of Jesus Christ. I try to teach my children to pray in the name of Jesus. Our power comes from no one else. It gives honor to our Savior when we acknowledge His sacrifice and pray in His name.

Just a little note to moms—Do the best you can. God knows your heart. Just stopping to lie on the floor in your bedroom to pray while the kids watch a video or play beside you is a beautiful act of obedience. Right this minute I am lying on the floor in my walk-in closet. The door is closed and my laptop is in here with me. All the kids are home for the summer. It's raining today, so they're inside. The boys have three friends over, and they're playing down the hall. I hear the phone ringing. Someone just knocked on the front door. The point is—we just have to pray anyway.

At least four people came in the closet while I was praying. "Sorry, Mom, but can we go to Caleb's house?" "What time is my appointment at the eye doctor?" "Why is your computer in here while you're praying?" I imagine God smiles. We're praying. He's listening and teaching little hearts at the same time. What a beautiful offering.

Tomorrow we're talking about fasting in secret. Don't skip it, okay? I am planning on fasting solid food in secret tomorrow (except you're reading about it later). I'd like for you to fast too. From what can you fast? One or two meals? Television? The telephone? What can you leave off tomorrow as we prepare to seek the heart of God through His call to fast?

Our fasting is supposed to have purpose. We'll fast together tomorrow, but start praying now about your individual purpose in fasting.

DAY 3

FASTING IN SECRET

At the end of yesterday's study I asked you to think about what you could fast from today. If you forgot about it, now it's time to decide. If you're doing this study in a group, they will know you are fasting, but other than those women, keep it a secret.

I remember having fasting days in seminary. Nobody called to ask me if I'd like to fast that particular day. But we were learning the discipline by practicing. The campus fast wasn't required, but it was strongly suggested. We all fasted together and whined a little, but, even so, God met with us powerfully. Sometimes we only grow in the disciplines of obedience because someone pushed us. As students we came to realize the value of the discipline and then began choosing it on our own.

From what have you chosen to fast today? _____

" 'When you fast, put oil on your head, and wash your face, so that you do not show your fasting to people but to your Father who is in secret. And your Father who sees in secret will reward you.' "
Matthew 6:17-18

Think about your personal, private purpose in our fast. The primary focus of fasting is always to center your heart on God. I'll ask you to write about yours at the end of today's study.

As with Jesus' other words on a secret life, Jesus doesn't say "If you fast," or "You have to fast." He says, " 'When you fast.' " These words, along with His other instructions, seem to clearly imply that a follower of Christ will fast as well as give and pray.

Who is Jesus talking to in Matthew 9:15 ?

_____

When did Jesus say that the disciples would fast?

_____

What happened in Acts 1:9?

_____

Jesus made it clear that He expected His disciples to fast after He was taken from them. His ascension obviously happened in Acts. Jesus did not give a strict command, but the principle is clear: Children who belong to the kingdom will practice the discipline of fasting.Let's walk through some of the spiritual purposes of fasting.[2]

Fasting centers our hearts on God. In the Sermon on the Mount, Jesus is most concerned with the motive in our fasting. Just a few minutes ago, I was getting some cereal for William and went to the pantry. Out of habit I began scanning the shelves to see if there was anything there I wanted. My head reminded me, *Oh yeah, I'm not eating today. Why aren't you eating? I want to hear more deeply from God for this study. Okay, close the door.*

All through the day, every little hunger pang, and every time I don't eat, I am reminded why. The why is about God. Let fasting do that for you today. Allow this day of gracious abstaining to center your heart on God. As I mentioned earlier, the primary purpose in fasting is to more fully focus on God, but there are also some secondary purposes.

In the margin write out a centering prayer, committing to put aside distraction for a day and look more intently for God.

> *The only ones who should know you are fasting are those who have to know. If you call attention to your fasting, people will be impressed and, as Jesus said, that will be your reward.*[1]

Fasting reveals the things that control us. Through food and other means, we cover up what is inside. Be prepared for things you have stuffed down to surface during a fast. Anger. Pride. Envy. Fear. As your fast reveals what has been covered, humbly accept the prompting to take that struggle to God for healing.

**Is fasting revealing things that control you? ❑ yes ❑ no
What kinds of things are you discovering? Underline all that apply.**

Pride	Envy	Family	Friends
Anger	Deceit	Appearance	Material possessions
Fear	Anxiety	Selfishness	Need to Control
Food	Money	Relationships	Other: _____

Fasting reminds us that God sustains us.

Turn to Matthew 4:4 and write the words of Jesus.

_____

_____

One of the reasons we are not to act miserable during our fast is because we are being nourished by the power of God. Fasting helps us keep our balance in life. Richard Foster writes: "How easily we begin to allow nonessentials to take precedence in our lives. How quickly we crave things we do not need until we are enslaved by them. … Our human cravings and desires are like rivers that tend to overflow their banks; fasting helps keep them in their proper channels."[3]

Fasting is a discipline and discipline helps keep balance in our lives. In the same way exercise is a discipline that brings balance to the physical body, fasting brings balance to the soul.

If you feel out of balance spiritually or emotionally, how do you think fasting might restore that balance?

_____

Numerous people have written on the many other values of fasting such as increased effectiveness in intercessory prayer, guidance in decisions, increased concentration, deliverance for those in bondage, physical well-being, revelations, and so on. In this, as in all matters, we can expect God to reward those who diligently seek Him.[4]

Today is only an introduction to fasting. As I write, I am praying that God will truly bless your day. I am asking Him to increase your commitment to this secret discipline. I hope you feel stretched spiritually.

How did God speak to you about your own personal purpose in today's fast?

_____

_____

_____

I humbled my soul with fasting.
Psalm 69:10, RSV

I fast for many reasons—as part of my fellowship with Christ; specific direction regarding one of my children; as I am writing to pursue a deeper intimacy with God; or when I am confused personally, usually in some matter that relates to my heart.

I haven't ever wanted to fast, so every time I am prompted to fast I am certain it's the Holy Spirit. When fasting comes to mind, I am usually certain why, but if not, I begin to ask God, "How do you want me to pray?" and "What is my purpose?"

Many others attest that fasting brings spiritual breakthroughs that cannot happen any other way. I pray your experience with this discipline will be the same.

Day 4

Where You Want Your Heart to Be

It seems like I spend most of my time accumulating earthly treasure. I provide for a family of five. A certain amount of earthly treasure is required to care for their bodies and their minds. Accumulating enough can necessitate huge amounts of effort and time.

I've tried to instruct my little ones in the discipline of fasting, and still they wake up wanting to eat every single day, no less than three times plus

" 'Don't collect for yourselves treasures on earth, where moth and rust destroy, and where thieves break in and steal. But collect for yourselves treasures in heaven, where neither moth nor rust destroys, and where thieves don't break in and steal. For where your treasure is, there your heart will be also.' "

Matthew 6:19-21

snacks. They have outgrown their school uniform shirts from last year, and I just realized that three of four have no appropriate shoes beyond flip-flops. Classes begin in two weeks and we just picked up the supply lists yesterday. Next week I'll wrangle the herd down to the store, feel great anxiety over finding the right color folders with pockets but without prongs, and then make my annual contribution toward the school supply treasure.

I do have it better than most working moms. I work at home. Which means when I can't think of something to write, I fold a load of towels. But even so, I'm sure the children feel like I'm working all the time just to acquire treasure that's going to rot and decay. That's why this passage is so important. And why it's so hard. And why it matters that we find a way to stockpile treasure where we want our hearts to be.

What do you think would be considered treasure in heaven? How about large accounts of forgiveness given? Drawers full of grace extended. A mattress stuffed with sacrifice and service and goodness. A cookie jar brimming with memories made and hugs given and tender looks across crowded rooms. A safe-deposit box packed with the secret life you have devoted to God. Maybe there is an old moving box stuffed with contentment. A scrapbook full of the joy you accumulated on the journey. And love— wouldn't it be great to need a garage just to hold all the love?

For the past few days I've made dinner. Not the regular, half take-out/half microwave kind of dinners. They've been sit-on-the-back-porch-and-snap-green-beans kind of dinners. Summer has such great food and I don't want my kids to miss it with their heads inside another pizza box. But I don't really have time for all this. My neighbor came over and gave me the royal rebuke, "Angela, you have a deadline. Why are you cooking these meals?"

I answered from my determination to find a balance, "The kids are my treasures. I want to store up blessings with them. They are worth more than a million books written, and they love it when I cook for them. If I fail at being their mom, nothing else really matters."

Every time I decide it's time to store up treasure in heaven, I am making a conscious decision to sacrifice treasure on earth. Maybe it's the treasure of a clean house, or the treasure of leisure, or the treasure I deposit into the bank. There is always a trade off. I ask God to give me a righteous balance. I need a Holy Spirit siren to go off inside my heart when I have not attended to kingdom treasure.

Stop and pray for that balance in your life. Your details may be very different, but I imagine that staying centered is difficult for you as well. Write your prayer in the margin.

Read Luke 12:13-21 and answer the following questions.

In verse 15, what does Jesus warn against?_____

What does God call the man who is only concerned with building

bigger barns? _____

In this parable, we learn that it's more important to:

_____

As you consider "storing up treasure in heaven," what kind of treasure comes to mind first?

_____

Where do you want your heart to be?

❑ I want my heart to be here on earth, focused on accumulation.
❑ I want both—earthly treasure and heavenly treasure.
❑ I want the balance. Enough earthly treasure to provide.
  Storehouses of heavenly wealth.

How do we lead the heart with our treasure? For me, the mandate to work hard and meet the needs of my pumpkins is a mandate. I am required to provide for them and I want to. But a few things can happen as I begin to apply this passage more aptly.

Sometimes we have to stop everything else and focus on what matters most. Your neighbor might not understand. Your coworkers probably won't get it. But if a Holy Spirit siren goes off in your head, respond quickly.

More often, I am looking for opportunities to build into heaven while I work here on earth. For me that might mean taking my kids on the road, even when it's inconvenient; staying up late to talk to my kid's friend for two hours; or missing a really great speaking opportunity for a family reunion.

On earth there is a place called "good enough." Do you know of it? There are good enough cars and good enough homes and good enough clothes. The people who store up treasure in heaven know all about good enough. Having good enough on earth, leaves a lot more time and energy for kingdom riches.

If God asked you to live in "good enough," how would that change the way you live now or the goals you have for the future?

_____

If your heart has been heavy, if you feel undue pressure or stress, if most days find you anxious and insecure, ask yourself, *Where is my treasure? Am I truly accumulating in heaven?* Your heart will follow your treasure and the heart that belongs to heaven finds a contentment we can't buy on this earth.

" ' Don't worry about your life, what you will eat or what you will drink; or about your body, what you will wear. Isn't life more than food and the body more than clothing?' "
Matthew 6:25

DAY 5

EXPECTING GOD

Read the verses in the margin. Underline everything Jesus tells us not to worry about. Now circle each reason He gives not to worry. Put a big box around what Jesus asks us to do instead of worry.

As you begin to live your life as a beautiful offering, here's what God is asking: do everything you can do to "seek first the kingdom" and then expect His divine provision for "all these things."

What does Hebrews 11:1 tell you about faith?

_____

" 'Don't worry about tomorrow, because tomorrow will worry about itself. Each day has enough trouble of its own.' "
Matthew 6:34

Faith is trusting in what we cannot see. It's the kind of faith God requires. But most of us worry when we can't see. Henry Blackaby says that when you can see, no faith is required. Faith is believing even when you cannot see.

There is a big life in front of you. You've made a few plans like I have, but who really knows? Everything in front of us is dark. But from the darkness, God keeps calling us toward the sound of His voice. And the voice of God speaks through His Son, Jesus, to specifically tell us to: *Seek Me first. Keep moving toward the kingdom. Live like you belong to the kingdom and trust Me. Don't worry. I know what you need. I know when you need.*

" 'Seek first the kingdom of God and His righteousness, and all these things will be provided for you.'
*"***Matthew 6:33**

What kinds of things are on the top of your worry list?

_____

Are there areas that move beyond worry and just seem impossible to you? If so, what are they?

_____

Look back over the things you've written down. What is God's instruction to you?

_____

Put your impossible alongside God's promise in Philippians 4:6:

_____ (your name), do not worry about

_____.

Instead, _____.

When I don't know what to do, I lean into Matthew 6:33 and ask myself, *How can I seek the kingdom in this moment? How can I pursue righteousness?* When you don't know what to do, seek God. Take the next blind step toward His voice. Keep going. Stop and hear His voice, then take another step.

It may be dark in front of you, but if you turn around I bet you'll be astounded by the glory of God's light. When I look back at the last 41 years, there is such a profound testimony of God's faithfulness. I have always had more than I truly need. He has worked in all things for good.

As you look back at God's faithfulness, how does that encourage you to trust Him with your future?

_____

When you belong to God, you have the privilege of expecting what other's cannot see or imagine. I can't tell you how many naysayers I've met on this journey. People want to steal your dreams and soak up your last drop of joy. So many of them have this way of encouraging worry, like maybe you're missing something if you don't worry with the same intensity they have.

I don't know what God will do. I only know what He has already done. I belong to the God who divided a sea to let His people through. I belong to the God who makes a new path through the desert. I belong to the God who built a bridge from heaven to earth just for me.

I cannot see how to navigate what seems impossible, but I will keep walking. I do not know how all these needs will be met, but I will trust with each mile marker of His faithfulness that God will give greater provision than I can imagine.

I will stand up and go forward and expect the bridge of His deliverance. A bridge of grace. An amazing superstructure of His glory where there seems to be no way. Is God asking you to expect a bridge across the very path that seems impossible?

Read the following passages from the prophet Isaiah. Underline the words or phrases that affirm God's faithfulness to you.

For I, the LORD your God,
hold your right hand
and say to you: Do not fear,
I will help you (Isaiah 41:13).

I will lead the blind by a way they did not know;
I will guide them on paths they have not known.
I will turn darkness to light in front of them,
and rough places into level ground.
This is what I will do for them,
and I will not forsake them (Isaiah 42:16).

The LORD will always lead you,
satisfy you in a parched land,
and strengthen your bones.
You will be like a watered garden
and like a spring whose waters never run dry (Isaiah 58:11).

God is asking you to rest and finally lay down your worry, but if you are new to faith you can't look back to a history of God's faithfulness. I want to encourage you to meet with another woman in your small-group study who's been walking with God for many years. Ask her to tell you how God has built bridge after bridge across her impossible times. Listen to the peace in her voice as she remembers all God has done and every need He has met.

Expect a bridge, my friend. You belong to God and you can safely lay down your worry.

---

[1]Richard Foster, *Celebration of Discipline: The Path to Spiritual Growth* (San Francisco: HarperSanFrancisco, 1988), 57-58.
[2]Ibid, 54-56.
[3]Ibid, 56.
[4]Ibid.

SESSION SIX ❧ VIEWER GUIDE

" 'Therefore everyone who hears these words of mine and puts them into practice is like a wise man who built his house on the rock. The rain came down, the streams rose, and the winds blew and beat against that house; yet it did not fall, because it had its foundation on the rock. But everyone who hears these words of mine and does not put them into practice is like a foolish man who built his house on sand. The rain came down, the streams rose, and the winds blew and beat against that house, and it fell with a great crash.' " **Matthew 7:24-27**

Build your life on the _____ of God's love for you.

"I am the true vine, and my Father is the gardener. He cuts off every branch in me that bears no fruit, while every branch that does bear fruit he prunes so that it will be even more fruitful. You are already clean because of the word I have spoken to you. Remain in me, and I will remain in you. No branch can bear fruit by itself; it must remain in the vine. Neither can you bear fruit unless you remain in me.

"I am the vine; you are the branches. If a man remains in me and I in him, he will bear much fruit; apart from me you can do nothing. If anyone does not remain in me, he is like a branch that is thrown away and withers; such branches are picked up, thrown into the fire and burned. If you remain in me and my words remain in you, ask whatever you wish, and it will be given you. This is to my Father's glory, that you bear much fruit, showing yourselves to be my disciples.

"As the Father has loved me, so have I loved you. Now remain in my love." **John 15:1-9**

To live the life Jesus dreamed for you, lay _____ on His altar.

HE'LL RAISE YOU UP

Father God, In this last week of study, remind us

that Your truth never ends. There is always

more with You. Let this just be the

beginning of our transformation.

A life that is becoming, growing,

and changing into Your likeness.

A heart that is being healed.

A soul that yearns for more.

Where the way is narrow, let us walk
with a righteous confidence. Where we have
given judgment, let us lay it down with humility.
Where the foundation is sinking sand, let us
tear down and rebuild on solid rock. Make us
amazing women with profound and amazing lives.
Every time someone looks toward us, let them
see Jesus. In our brokenness. In our accomplishment.
In our obedience. In our forgiveness. Make us women
who reflect Your grace with passion.

Take each day and give wisdom. Open our eyes and
soften our hearts. Lead us by Your Holy Spirit. Make this life
a beautiful offering.

Because of Jesus and His love, Amen.

WEEK SIX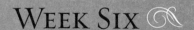

DAY 1

LAY IT DOWN

"Do not judge, so that you won't be judged. For with the judgment you use, you will be judged, and with the measure you use, it will be measured to you" (Matt. 7:1-2).

As you read this passage, what tone do you hear Jesus using?

❑ warning   ❑ encouraging
❑ rewarding   ❑ teaching
❑ threatening   ❑ other: _____

> *We must beware of believing that it is okay for us to condemn as long as we are condemning the right things. It is not so simple as all that. I can trust Jesus to go into the temple and drive out those who were profiting from religion, beating them with a rope. I cannot trust myself to do so.*
> —*Dallas Willard* [1]

I tend to think Jesus was fired up as He spoke. People don't come to know Jesus as their Savior because they've been judged. Wounds don't find healing through judgment. Marriages can never be judged into restoration. Baby Christians don't become mature believers because they have been judged.

Does any good happen because we allow ourselves to become judgmental or come through the door with a negative spirit? I've never seen one heart mended in judgment. It encourages no one. Receiving sustained criticism, condemnation, or painful words doesn't motivate change. Why is it so much easier to find fault? Why do people spend huge amounts of energy and emotion being negative? What if they tried just one time to see things differently? Decided to bite their tongues instead of speaking recklessly? Worked on getting the planks out of their own eye first? (See Matthew 7:3-5 in the margin.)

Why do you think we are so inclined to judge the sins of others while overlooking our own?

_____

Sadly, our plank of judgment often keeps us from helping others with the speck of their sin. Imagine what it would feel like to just lay down our judgment and begin to love others as freely as Jesus does.

Like Jesus, this topic gets me fired up! Misinformed, careless judgment ought to get us riled up. It serves no purpose in the kingdom of heaven. We have so much more to do with our lives. Jesus said not to judge. It tarnishes our beautiful offering.

" 'Why do you look at the speck of sawdust in your brother's eye and pay no attention to the plank in your own eye? How can you say to your brother, "Let me take the speck out of your eye," when all the time there is a plank in your own eye? You hypocrite, first take the plank out of your own eye, and then you will see clearly to remove the speck from your brother's eye.' "
Matthew 7:3-5, NIV

I care very little if I am judged by you or by any human court; indeed, I do not even judge myself. My conscience is clear, but that does not make me innocent. It is the Lord who judges me. Therefore judge nothing before the appointed time; wait till the Lord comes. He will bring to light what is hidden in darkness and will expose the motives of men's hearts. At that time each will receive his praise from God.
1 Corinthians 4:3-5, NIV

Speak and act as those who will be judged by the law of freedom. For judgment is without mercy to the one who hasn't shown mercy Mercy triumphs over judgment.
James 2:12-13

Read the verses in the margin and answer the following questions.

According to 1 Corinthians 4:3-5, what should we judge?

_____

Fill in these blanks.
God will bring to light _____

and will expose _____.

How does James 2:12-13 say we are supposed to speak and act?

_____

Remember the call to be merciful earlier in this sermon (Matt. 5:7)? When one has been judged and then given freedom, they have been given mercy.

_____ **triumphs over** _____!

In this sermon, Jesus has given us many gracious instructions. Sometimes He has asked us to put on a kingdom attitude that bears His likeness. Other times, He directs us to choose attributes and actions that reflect the heart of the Father. But here, Jesus uses stronger language to require us to lay something down. He wants us to lay down our judgment, our critical spirit, our negativity, our disapproval. He wants us to give it up—permanently.

Do you have a natural inclination toward negativity or judgment? How is God speaking to you through the words of Jesus regarding your attitude?

_____

The life God wants for you and me doesn't contain even a hint of judgment. He isn't talking about discernment or wisdom in regard to judging circumstances or discerning truth from error.

How would you distinguish between judging and rejecting falsehood?

_____

This instruction is a lesson on condemnation. Jesus never gives us permission to condemn others.

Jesus calls the one inclined to condemnation a hypocrite. The hypocrite is easy to spot in this context because her condemning spirit always gives her away. The mere fact that we have become judgmental is the first clue that we do not have the kingdom heart Jesus has been talking about in this passage. The judgmental spirit has companions in anger, contempt, and self-righteousness. The woman who is quick to judge finds herself blind to the humanity and heart of other people.

As I thought through this and saw parts of my own life that had to change, I realized I cannot simply judge others less or judge others more fairly. I need to go with the directive in Jesus' instruction. Judge not. Lay it down. Just give up the whole judgment thing and let God take care of it.

Tomorrow we'll talk more about the woman who lives without judgment. It's very cool to start living in that kind of freedom. I promise, as soon as you begin tasting a life without quick judgment, you'll never want to go back to the bitter woman.

May God yank us all away from the tendency toward judgment. May we become women who triumph because of mercy!

Do not criticize one another, brother. He who criticizes against a brother or judges his brother criticizes the law and judges the law. But if you judge the law, you are not a doer of the law, but a judge. There is only one lawgiver and judge who is able to save and to destroy. But who are you to judge your neighbor?
James 4:11-12

Day 2

Giving No Condemnation

Over and over in this sermon, Jesus asks us to give to others what the Father has already lavished upon us. He wants us to live like we belong to the kingdom of God. Reflecting the light of His glory into darkness. Bringing the power of His indwelling right into the middle of our everyday lives and our everyday family. Giving His no condemnation in place of the world's judgment.

Is there someone in your life who needs to know that "no condemnation now exists" from Jesus and from you? Write the name(s) or initials below.

No condemnation now exists for those in Christ Jesus.
Romans 8:1

_____

I met a couple of teenage girls a few months ago. They came to our family as the friends of a friend. And I have to tell you, I am struggling. These girls aren't really the kind of girls I'd planned on having around the house. They aren't the ones I'd hand-pick to hang out with my children. I have worked with students for almost 20 years. With those years comes the ability to look into the eyes of a kid and read the heart. When I look into the eyes of these two girls, I see darkness, insecurity, anger, rebellion. My heart is tender toward them, but my children are my cubs and I am the mama-bear. I just wanted these girls to go away.

So, guess who came over last night? The girls I don't want around. Guess what God is doing? Convicting my heart. Turns out both girls have been reared in the dark. Neither has parents that pay attention to them. Oblivious is the word they used to describe their moms. Both have already made some incredibly rotten choices at 14. Neither understands consequences, but I can see that freight train barreling straight for them.

I sat the girls down and talked to them about the way I parent and my responsibility to God to be a protector. They looked at me like I was crazy when I told them about the Holy Spirit siren that goes off in my mother heart when something is weird. And when I was done with the sermon part, I told them I want them to be protected too. I told them about mercy and starting over. I realized they needed to hear God and no condemnation in the same sentence. They cried. My daughter cried. I felt like I had carried the light of Christ into their darkness. We'll see how they choose to respond.

Laying down your judgment seems to go pretty smoothly when it's someone far, far away or an event long, long ago. But Jesus said these ideas are supposed to radically impact your life this very day. The way you talk to the people who sleep beside you. The attitude you have on your drive into work. The decisions you make in the secret of your heart. The way you embrace the unlovely who show up on your door.

What if, instead of judgment, we came alongside people in their pain and took them by the hand and into the presence of God? What if we stayed with them until they had been introduced to the only One who can forgive and heal and restore? What if we weren't afraid of their past? What if the people who came into your life felt no condemnation?

How would you rate the way others feel in your presence?

1	2	3	4	5	6	7	8	9	10

Most are keenly aware of my judgment.

I have laid down my judgment.

Have you experienced the truth of Romans 8:1 in your life?
❑ yes ❑ no

How do you believe God is asking you to use that truth in the relationship(s) you listed on page 91?

_____

We have been wounded. We have been the victims of senseless actions. It seems like somebody should pay for all the pain we've felt. We feel entitled to stand in condemnation. Here's where this gets more difficult. Even if we are entitled, Jesus still asks us to lay it down. Surrender our right to judge. Humble ourselves before the Creator. Trust in His authority and wisdom. Allow Him to unfold circumstances over time. He has full jurisdiction. Let God demonstrate His sovereign rule, both in your heart and through your life. Trust the Father to be your protector.

You have not received condemnation from Christ. Don't you think it's time to give no condemnation? What if your husband comes home tonight and he gets no condemnation? What if your son asks you to sign his English paper with a D, and he receives no condemnation?

What if you wake up in the morning and for the first time don't beat yourself up for every stupid thing you've ever done? What if the truth of no condemnation lets you become a new woman? What if this whole idea sets you free?

Yesterday we talked about becoming women who triumph because of mercy. The more I lay down my judgment, the more freedom I know. My stomach doesn't hurt. I can sleep at night. I am not plotting revenge. I am resting in the truth of God as final Judge. I get to give out the goodness He has given to me.

Have you ever had one of those moments when you expected someone to completely explode? You wound your heart tightly in a ball and waited for the thrashing. But there was nothing, so you waited a little longer. Still nothing. After a time you realized the punishment you anticipated wasn't coming. Do you remember how that felt? Relief. Sweet relief.

That's how people will feel as this truth is set free to transform your life. They will find relief in your presence. They will taste through you what the Father longs to give them through His Son.

Would you commit this day to lay it all down? What if you spend the rest of your life without a big plank of judgment in your eyes?

You'll be able to see.

You'll see God.

With the arrival of Jesus, the Messiah, that fateful dilemma is resolved. Those who enter into Christ's being-here-for-us no longer have to live under a continuous, low-lying black cloud. A new power is in operation. The Spirit of life in Christ, like a strong wind has magnificently cleared the air, freeing you from a fated lifetime of brutal tyranny at the hands of sin and death.
Romans 8:1-2,
The Message

And you'll see the ones He loves.
And you'll see where He'd like for you to be.

Spend some time in prayer. Verbalize your commitment to the Lord to lay down judgment. Thank Him for the peace you are promised will come.

DAY 3

THE NARROW WAY

Enter through the narrow gate. For wide is the gate and broad is the road that leads to destruction, and many enter through it. But small is the gate and narrow the road that leads to life, and only a few find it.
Matthew 7:13-14, NIV

I have a teenage daughter. She is beautiful and sweet and very social. She loves God, but I know Satan wants to take her out, so we have a "come to Jesus" meeting every few days. I am good at talking, a trait I inherited from my father, and she has become very good at listening.

I remember the endless listening of my teenage years, and I can watch Taylor's eyes glaze over in exactly the same way mine did. She nods like she hears me and throws in polite smiling when I'm funny, just like I did when my daddy would sit us down for a talk. My friends would always try to hurry out when they felt one of those extended sermons coming. It never worked. He told them to sit down. A couple of hours later we were too tired from all that listening to get into trouble.

Here's what I've been saying to Taylor lately, "I don't want you to have a testimony people will pay to hear. I don't want you to have a big story to tell. I don't want you standing in front of some group of women when you're 35 saying, 'Well it all started when I was a teenager. Somehow I began hanging around the wrong people. Everybody else was doing it, so I did. I totally ruined my life, but Jesus still loves me and that's what I'm here to tell you.'

"Here's what I hope you get to say instead, 'God got a hold of me early. I decided to believe everything He had written to me was true. I decided to live like I belong to the kingdom. Proverbs says blessing comes from obedience and the disobedient suffer consequences. I haven't been perfect, but I keep trying to be obedient and God has really blessed my life.' Boring. No one will ever pay to hear that."

I think the whole narrow gate and narrow road thing has gotten a bad rap. We assume it means boring. Like we could miss out on something if we go that way. What most people don't understand is that the narrow road leads to blessing.

Fill in the blanks based on Matthew 7:13-14.

Wide is the gate and broad is the road that leads to _____.

Small is the gate and narrow the road that leads to _____.

Read John 10:9 What does Jesus call Himself? _____

What happens to the person who enters through Jesus?

_____

Now read John 14:6. How many ways are there to be saved?

_____

" 'I am the door. If anyone enters by Me, he will be saved.' "
John 10:9

" 'I am the way, the truth, and the life. No one comes to the Father except through Me.' "
John 14:6

From these verses, we can conclude that the narrow gate is Jesus Himself and entering through the narrow gate means coming to Jesus Christ for your salvation. He is the only entrance into eternity. Every other way leads to destruction and death. Every other gate is a dead end. There are no shortcuts to God.

On the other side of the narrow gate is the narrow road. This is where most of us are right now. We have come to know Jesus as our Savior and it's time to walk down the narrow path. Some of you have been going along with me but you feel like the narrow road is beginning to close in. You feel like you have to give up too much. You might even feel mad.

The narrow road is not narrow-mindedness.

The narrow road is not a list of rules to be kept.

The narrow road is not doctrinal correctness.

The narrow road is not a lonely road.

The narrow road is not fraught with haughtiness, television evangelists, and street-corner, Bible-thumping screamers.

The narrow road is not the opposite of everything good and fun and desirable.

According to John 14:21,23, if we love Jesus we will ...

_____

The narrow road is obedience. It is the characteristic of a woman who loves God.

" 'If you continue in My word, you really are My disciples. You will know the truth, and the truth will set you free.' "
John 8:31-32

Read John 8:31-32 . Underline what happens to the woman who follows the teaching of Jesus and applies that truth to her life? How do you define obedience in your relationship with God? Check all that apply.

❑ submissive	❑ weak willed	❑ compliant
❑ yielding	❑ loyal	❑ willful
❑ devoted	❑ freeing	❑ resigned
❑ teachable	❑ respectful	❑ other: _____

Freedom comes from obedience. Obedience is not perfection. Obedience is the road you walk when you decide to live out the teachings of Jesus. The road is narrow because there aren't too many people on it. On the narrow road, you are walking underneath the anointing of God. It's powerful there. You stay right in the middle of His big dreams for you. You are kept on the path by the guardrails of His protection. And on this road, you're free.

Most people think the 10-lane interstate looks a lot more interesting than this narrow road. What they don't know is wide path living goes nowhere with God. There is only one way. The narrow way. It leads to blessing. And with blessing, comes kingdom abundance.

Have you ever regretted obeying God? ❑ yes ❑ no

If yes, explain. _____

_____

Have you ever regretted not obeying God? ❑ yes ❑ no

If yes, explain. _____

_____

In obedience, I've felt very uncomfortable. I've been embarrassed. I've felt unsure in the moment. But I have never regretted obeying God. I can look back at my life without a headline testimony and see God's blessing all over.

Even in your weakness and humanity, God desires to pour His abundance over your obedience. Even when you are broken, even when you don't think you are enough, even when you are persecuted, even then, your obedience brings His blessing.

As you pray today, walk back with God and remember His blessings. Specifically try to remember the blessings that have come attached to your obedience.

When you and I decide to obey, we decide to trust that God knows more. Humble your heart and choose the narrow road of obedience and trust that is waiting for you in the kingdom abundance of God's blessing.

DAY 4

BUILD ON THE ROCK

Once upon a time a woman went to a lot of Bible studies. For nine years she had gone to one with piles of homework that met at the big church across town. All her friends went and the society women from the club went, so she did too. In addition to the big Bible study, she bounced around to some other studies, the kind with only a little homework and videos to watch. All her neighborhood friends came to those and someone brought breakfast, so she went too.

The Bible study woman liked her life. She liked seeing her friends. The things they talked about during the meetings were spiritual and good when they stayed on track. The workbook forced her to open her Bible a few times a week. The prayer time kept her up to speed with everyone's life. The Bible study woman always felt good when she left another meeting. She liked feeling good.

But one day, the Bible study woman got some devastating news. It would have been difficult for anyone to hear. The shock made her feel like the earth was crumbling and everything underneath her was washing away. And the Bible study woman didn't know what to do. She cried and cried but couldn't find her bearings. Eventually her desperate soul sank deep into despair.

All her Bible study friends came to see the Bible study woman. They brought her food and prayed with her and told her God would help. But the woman could not find peace. She had learned a lot of Bible words and sung all the Jesus songs and bowed her head while people prayed, but the Bible study woman didn't really know God. All those years she had been building on sand. When the winds came and the waters rose, she helplessly watched as it all washed away.

What about this story struck home with you?

_____

We are at the end of Jesus' teaching in the Sermon on the Mount. These last verses about building on the rock instead of the sand give us His final instruction, the summary of His sermon, and the reason it all matters.

Look at the verses in the margin. What is the difference between the wise man and the foolish man?

_____

" 'Everyone who hears these words of mine and puts them into practice is like a wise man who built his house on the rock. The rain came down, the streams rose, and the winds blew and beat against that house; yet it did not fall, because it had its foundation on the rock.' "
Matthew 7:24-25, NIV

Obviously you come to Bible studies. You have faithfully worked through this study. You pray or at least pray along when others pray. But how are you building—like the wise or like the foolish?

We assume that attending and hearing is practicing, but it's not. None of this really matters if your life is not being transformed by the truths you've learned.

Next I'm going to ask you some questions. Please don't skip over them. Prayerfully consider each one before you respond. You will not be asked to share these answers in your small-group meeting. This is between you and God.

Where can you see God's sculpting and refining hand in your life right now?

_____

" 'Everyone who hears these words of mine and does not put them into practice is like a foolish man who built his house on sand.' "
Matthew 7:26, NIV

Name a specific new truth that is changing an old behavior or attitude.

_____

What is standing between you and change? A specific hidden sin? A lazy heart? What is it that keeps you from a full-life commitment?

_____

I knew a man who signed up for three years of intense discipleship through his church. He met with a group of seven men every Tuesday morning at 6:00 a.m. for two hours. At the end of three years, the group had a celebration dinner. After dinner, the man went home to his wife, beaming with pride over his accomplishment. Three years of vigorous study and accountability. He was bubbling with enthusiasm. His wife stood in the kitchen and listened. When he was done, she offered without emotion, "You'd think all that Bible study would make a difference in the way you live your life."

Do the people closest to you truly see God transforming your life? Softening your heart? Reshaping your countenance? Ask a family member what he or she sees God doing in your life. Record his or her response below.

_____

_____

I love that it's never too late to become the woman you have always wanted to be. Maybe you have built on sand in the past, but you can start over. You can build your life on the rock of Jesus.

Let us hold on to the confession of our hope without wavering, for He who promised is faithful.
Hebrews 10:23

Describe the woman you have always wanted to be.

_____

_____

He who started a good work in you will carry it on to completion until the day of Christ Jesus.
Philippians 1:6

Maybe they just see a Bible in your back seat. Some papers scattered around the house. A woman who has one more Jesus thing on her to-do list. An attitude that's been the same for 20 years.

My dear sister, we can return God's love to us with our lives. We can bless Him with an offering that He calls beautiful. We can decide to turn our lives in the direction of God and stay faithful to look toward Him until we see Him face-to-face. No matter where you have been or how much trouble you have known, your life can become a strong house built on the solid foundation of Jesus Christ. You can become a wise woman who puts the words of God into practice in her life.

Pray. Consider where you are. Ask God for His powerful wisdom.

Did I tell you I love you for hanging in here? I do.

DAY 5

AN AMAZING LIFE

Last week the kids and I returned from our annual beach vacation. One condo, my family plus my sister-in-law and her 4 boys. That would be 2 adult women and 8 kids. I know you're sorry you missed it. You could have come for the 2 days the other sister came. Then we were up to 3 women and 10 kids with some floor space to spare. Ever heard of needing a vacation after your vacation? The mamas both needed a vacation after 9 days of fun and sun.

All week long the kids were whining about going to the souvenir store. We put it off as long as possible for the obvious reasons. I'd almost rather give birth again than take that crew to a store where you walk through a big, fake shark's mouth to get to the flip-flops and painted driftwood and pop-guns. As free enterprise would have it, there isn't just one of those places, there's a million of them. In search of just the right beach scene snow globe, we went from Souvenir Pavilion to Souvenir World to Souvenir Palace. I thought I was going to die a slow death from overexposure to incense and tanning oil.

Here's what's really amazing to me. There are 4 million sunburned people in those stores, all buying the tackiest shell junk known to mankind. AnnaGrace bought a grass skirt and a bottle with some blue sand and plastic shells inside with the name of our beach stamped across the front. William bought a wooden sword (a decision I now regret, but it kept us from going to the Souvenir Emporium) with the same stamped name and Grayson bought a bottle with a boat inside.

I don't want you to leave this study about the Sermon on the Mount with some cheap, rinky-dink souvenir. We have spent weeks sprawled out beside the ocean of God's wisdom, basking in the radiance of His glory. I don't want you to take these truths home in a sweet little book and put it on the shelf so you can look at it's cover from time to time and remember God. Please don't let this become a Jesus souvenir. I have a better idea. Instead of little trinkets to remind us of where we've been, let's just move there.

I have a friend who lives on the beach in California. It must be one of the most beautiful places in the world. Every evening you can sit in his house with your chair facing a picture window and watch the sun set over the Pacific Ocean. It's absolutely breathtaking. If you get to choose where you live, why in the world would you choose any place else? And if you can spend everyday of your life living inside the kingdom of God's protection and blessing, how could you ever settle for a little souvenir remembrance instead?

In the Sermon on the Mount, Jesus has given us everything we need to lay the foundation for an amazing life. He has outlined all the characteristics of a beautiful offering.

Do you want a life that will stand firm against every trial and storm that comes against it? Do you want to return to God a beautiful offering? Do you want the glory of God to walk into the room with you?

We only get one life to build for His kingdom. That's why these living instructions in the Sermon on the Mount matter. That's why it matters that your life becomes a beautiful offering.

I believe that the best way for us to conclude is in a time of prayer. I'll guide you again. You pray and write as you feel led. First I want you to close your eyes and envision yourself being laid on the altar of God. Your life, your heart, your mind, and your countenance all laid down for His blessing.

According to Ephesians 5:1-2, how do we become imitators of God?

_____

Now express to God your desire to be a fragrant offering.

How does Romans 12:1 instruct us to offer ourselves to God?

_____

Now pray that back to God.

Read 2 Chronicles 16:9. From where does our strength come?

_____

Tell God about your thankfulness for His strength.

Read 2 Corinthians 3:5. From where does our competence come?

_____

Ask God for His continued wisdom.

Read Proverbs 10:6 and John 1:16. What do we receive for our right living?

_____

_____

Thank God for your blessings now and for the ones He has promised for the future. Ask Him for continued blessing and favor. Pray for your children's children, that they will receive blessing through your faithfulness.

Read the next passage out loud as a prayer back to God.

For I am persuaded that neither death not life,
neither angels nor rulers,
neither the present, nor things to come, nor powers,
nor height, nor depth, nor any other created thing,
will have the power to separate us
from the love of God that is in Christ Jesus our Lord! (Rom. 8:38-39).

Conclude your time of prayer with your own words of commitment, your own thoughts about love, and your own desire to live for the glory of God.

God bless you, dear one. I pray He blows the doors off of every dream you've ever had and shows you what dreaming really looks like. I pray the Sermon on the Mount will continue to work its way deep into your soul. I'm asking God to bless the offering of your life and make it beautiful.

Press on, my friend. Please don't ever give up. No matter what comes, just keep moving in the direction of God's voice. Keep trusting in the security of His embrace. God really calls you beautiful. Wallflowers really get to dance. And your life can really become beautiful to Him.

I love you. It has been a privilege to run alongside you for these weeks.

Angela

---

[1]Dallas Willard, *The Divine Conspiracy: Rediscovering Our Hidden Life in God* (San Francisco: HarperCollins Publishers, 1998), 221.

LEADER GUIDE

This leader guide will help you facilitate the small-group sessions for *Living Your Life as a Beautiful Offering*. A leader kit is also available (item 001260512) containing two DVDs with Angela's accompanying video messages to be used during the small-group sessions. While the video messages are valuable to the study, you may choose to do the study using only the member book.

If you are leading this study without the accompanying video messages, the introductory session is optional. Having an introductory session offers a time to distribute the member book and get acquainted. If you choose not to have an introductory session, make certain participants receive their workbooks in time to complete week 1 before group session 1.

If you are using the accompanying video messages in your study, offer an introductory session for all women who think they might be interested in participating in this study. No member book is needed for this session.

This leader guide also contains plans for an optional celebration session. This is a time when the women can come together, share food and fellowship, and discuss the things that have meant the most to them in their study of *Living Your Life as a Beautiful Offering*. For those groups using the videos, this session provides a time to show the bonus feature—A Conversation with Angela.

Ask God to put together the small group He desires for this study. Announce the study in the church newsletter, worship bulletin, on hallway bulletin boards, and at women's ministry activities. Use the promotional segment on DVD disc 1.

Secure child care for each session if necessary. Before each session arrange to have a DVD player in your meeting room. Complete each week's assignments. As the leader you do not have to have all the answers, but you need to be familiar with the material. This leader guide is designed to be used for a 60-90 minute small-group session. You can set the format and time frame of your group session based on how much time you wish to allow for discussion. Don't feel you have to cover every activity in this leader guide. Many more discussion starters are offered each week than you will be able to cover in a single session. Be flexible. Consider the personality of your group as you make decisions about which topics to discuss. Allow the Lord to lead your group discussions.

If your group is too large for meaningful discussion to take place, consider breaking into smaller groups of 4-6 for discussion and coming together as a larger group to view the video.

INTRODUCTORY SESSION

Before the Study
1. Read About the Author (p. 4) and About the Study (p. 6) and be prepared to introduce the author, the study, and the format.
2. Have copies of *Living Your Life as a Beautiful Offering* ready for distribution.
3. Make plans to have refreshments if you choose.

During the Session
1. Welcome the women as they arrive.
2. Introduce yourself and, depending on the familiarity of the group, give a little information about yourself. Create a casual, nonthreatening atmosphere for the women. Explain that this is an opportunity for them to get an introduction to Angela and her message. After this session they may choose whether or not they wish to continue in the next six weeks of study.
3. Introduce Angela Thomas and the message of the study.

4. Play the music video, "This Is My Offering."

5. Show the introductory video session, God Calls You Beautiful.

6. Have a time of reflection. Pose these questions, but don't ask for a response: *Do you doubt that God can use you—a broken woman? Are you standing around the edge of your life? Do you want to dance the dance of your life in His arms? If you've asked any of these questions, this study is for you! God made us for dancing! He is wild about us!*

7. Have a time of prayer. Ask God to help you live like you belong to Him. Thank Him for offering to you the dance of your life! Ask Him to help you return His love with your life. While continuing in prayer, play the music video again. Lead the women to spend some time praying silently, asking God His will for their participation in this study.

8. Explain the format of the study.

9. Give the women an opportunity to purchase member books. Assure them books will be available next week if they need more time to make a decision. If members are responsible for paying for their books, offer to collect the money.

10. Assign week 1 for the next small-group session. Encourage them to complete each learning activity to get the most out of this study.

SESSION 1

Before the Session

1. Prepare an attendance sheet for members to sign their names, addresses, phone numbers, and e-mail addresses. Place this sheet on a table with pens, markers, and nametags.

2. Have member books available for newcomers.

3. Have a chalkboard, poster board, or flipchart available.

4. Complete the week 1 material and view the session 1 video, A Beautiful Offering.

During the Session

1. As participants arrive, ask them to sign in, prepare nametags, and pick up copies of the member book if they don't already have theirs. Offer to collect the money.

2. Introduce yourself and, depending on the familiarity of the group, give a little information about yourself. Ask each member to do the same.

3. If you did not have an introductory session, introduce Angela Thomas and explain the message and format of the study. Explain that each week you will discuss the material each person has studied individually during the week. Encourage them to complete every learning activity to get the most out of their study.

4. Ask for volunteers to share why they chose to participate in this study.

5. Use the following for discussion:

a. Read Matthew 4:23-25 (p. 9) and discuss how people spread the word about Jesus. Ask: *Who influenced your thinking toward God? How has this person(s) shaped your relationship with God? Do you tell people about your compassionate Savior or righteous judge?* (p. 10)

b. Refer to the activity on page 12. Recreate the chart on the board and ask volunteers to call out the answers to fill in the blanks. Ask for volunteers to answer: *Which one of these blessings most directly speaks to where you are today and why?*

c. Ask, *What does being poor in spirit mean? Have you ever experienced poverty of spirit? How did it affect you? your relationships?* Remind participants how important it is to seek the presence of God during these times to fight the shadows of loneliness and the distraction of sin.

d. Ask someone to read 2 Corinthians 4:7-18. Ask, *What treasure has God given you because of your brokenness? What is the benefit of your brokenness and heartache?* (pp. 19-20)

  e. Ask someone to read the Henri Nouwen quote on page 21. Ask, *How does this change your actions and reactions in the area where you most need to know the comfort of God right now?*

6. Encourage participants to turn to the viewer guide on page 7 and take notes as they watch the video. Show video session 1, A Beautiful Offering.

7. Video reflection: Remind the women when there is little else they can choose, they can **always** choose where they look. Say, *If you took a trip to a distant land that cost you everything, it's never too late to turn your heart back toward the Father. Turn your gaze toward home. He's waiting.*

8. Close in prayer. Thank God for the assurance that He holds us up. He gives healing and hope when we call on His name. Thank Him for the treasure He makes from our heartaches.

9. Assign week 2 for the next small-group session.

SESSION 2

Before the Session

1. Have a chalkboard, poster board, or flipchart available.

2. Complete the week 2 material and view the session 2 video, The Cup of Your Soul.

During the Session

1. Welcome the women as they arrive.

2. Discuss feelings associated with physical hunger and thirst. Compare that with spiritual hunger and thirst.

3. Use the following for discussion:

  a. Recreate the chart on page 26. Meekness is … Meekness is not … Say, *When you and I lay our lives on the altar of God, we put ourselves*

inside the covering of Christ. That's meekness— that's where He takes meek women and makes them amazing!

  b. Ask, *How do you think you could increase your hunger for God?* List responses.

  c. Say, *Grayson asked to mow the yard and wasn't deterred by obstacles along the way.* Read through the "prayer" on page 32. Challenge women to "choose" rather than avoid those things that require effort or discipline.

  d. Write the attributes of God listed on pages 34-35 on the board—sovereign, unchangeable, omnipresent, omnipotent, truth, good, just, love, holy. Ask, *Which of these speak loudest to your doubts? Why?*

  e. Ask the women, *Do you have preconceived ideas about how God will or won't speak to you? Have these preconceptions hindered your hearing from Him? How?* Encourage them, *Make a conscious choice to watch and listen.*

4. Encourage participants to turn to the viewer guide on page 23 and take notes as they watch the video. Show video session 2, The Cup of Your Soul.

5. Video reflection: Emphasize to participants: *Don't settle for just a taste. Go for the feast!*

6. Close in prayer. Ask God to make you hungry and thirsty for Him. Ask Him to remove distractions that keep you from seeking Him and fill you with His presence.

7. Assign week 3 for the next small-group session.

SESSION 3

Before the Session

1. Have a chalkboard, poster board, or flipchart available.

2. Complete the week 3 material and view the session 3 video, God Delights to Show Mercy.

During the Session

1. Welcome the women as they arrive.

2. Ask, *What opportunities did you have this week to give away the mercy and grace you've been given?*

3. Use the following for discussion:

   a. Say, *Think of a time you received mercy from God or another person. How did receiving that mercy make you feel? Did it make you want to extend mercy to others?*

   b. Ask, *What is the blessing of a pure heart?* (to see God) Remind women that we can never attain and sustain purity—it's a moment-my-moment cleansing from God. And He never gets tired of us asking!

   c. Read through the list of observations about those who can see God (p. 47). Say, *Running toward His purity means asking God to do what you can't, praying for change in your attitude, and asking Him to do whatever it takes to clean what has been impure in your life. What's the blessing? We see Him! It's worth it!*

   d. Say, *Think of a woman you know who seems to radiate a heart and countenance of true peace. What characteristics describe her life?* (p. 50) List them on the board.

   e. Say, *When we follow the Lord, persecution is sure, even though we don't like to talk about it or even think about it. How can we prepare ourselves?* List responses on the board.

4. Encourage participants to turn to the viewer guide on page 39 and take notes as they watch the video. View video session 3, God Delights to Show Mercy.

5. Video reflection: Ask, *What are you dragging around? What are you hiding behind your back? What is your sack of ashes?*

6. Close in prayer, Pray that mercy walks in the room with you. Ask God for a holy confidence, even in the middle of attacks.

7. Assign week 4 for the next small-group session.

SESSION 4

Before the Session

1. Have a chalkboard, poster board, or flipchart available.

2. Complete the week 4 material and view the session 4 video, You Belong to Heaven.

During the Session

1. Welcome the women as they arrive.

2. Discuss, *Who do you belong to?*

3. Use the following for discussion:

   a. Say, *Angela shares that sometimes learning to trust God more feels like a free fall. She says, "Trusting is learning to breath during the fall."* Discuss what that means.

   b. Talk about how you each defined *grace* (p. 60). List responses to "Gods grace for my life means that …"

   c. Ask volunteers to share places they have an opportunity to be salt. Then ask, *How can you act that out?*

   d. Ask for a volunteer to read Matthew 5:15-16, *The Message*, (p. 66). Ask, *How would your life look different if you lived like this?*

   e. Ask, *What attitudes or behaviors get in the way of your obedience?* (p. 68) *Which is most difficult for you to surrender?* Have a time of silent prayer when the women can surrender the things the Lord is asking them to let go.

4. Encourage participants to turn to the viewer guide on page 55 and take notes as they watch the video. Show video session 4, You Belong to Heaven.

5. Video reflection: Ask, *Are you "taking it to the hoop"? Are you shining like a city on a hill?*

6. Close in prayer. Ask the Lord to help you trust Him more. Thank Him for His indescribable grace in your life. Ask Him to show you places you can be salt and light.

7. Assign week 5 for the next small-group session.

SESSION 5

Before the Session

1. Have a chalkboard, poster board, or flipchart available.
2. Complete the week 5 material and view the session 5 video, Keeping a Secret Life.

During the Session

1. Welcome the women as they arrive.
2. Discuss, *Think of times in your life when you've been asked to keep a secret. How hard was it?*
3. Use the following for discussion:
   a. Ask, *What are some creative ways to give in secret?* (p. 74) Make a list on the board.
   b. Ask, *What are some practical things you do to protect your secret place and the time you spend there?*
   c. Ask, *What things has the Lord shown you through fasting?*
   d. Ask, *What things can we do to store up treasures in heaven?*
   e. Ask, *What things cause you to worry? How has worry changed these things? Has God been faithful in this areas in the past? What does that tell you about the future?*
4. Encourage participants to turn to the viewer guide on page 71 and take notes as they watch the video. Show video session 5, Keeping a Secret Place.
5. Video reflection: Ask, *Are you living like God's Word is true? When you lie on your face and wait for God, do you expect Him to come?*
6. Close in prayer. Ask the Lord to strengthen your secret life with Him. Ask Him to help you carve out time to spend with Him in your secret place. Ask Him to make you more aware of opportunities to give in secret and of times He is calling you to fast something so that you might focus more on Him.
7. Assign week 6 for the next small-group session.

SESSION 6

Before the Session

1. Have a chalkboard, poster board, or flipchart available.
2. Complete the week 6 material and view the session 6 video, He'll Raise You Up.

During the Session

1. Welcome the women as they arrive.
2. Ask, *How is building a house on a poor foundation like building our spiritual lives on false ideas and wrong behaviors?*
3. Use the following for discussion:
   a. Ask for a volunteer to read the Dallas Willard quote on page 89. Discuss the quote as a group.
   b. Ask, *Do you know someone who needs to know "no condemnation"? How can you communicate that?*
   c. Read through the list of things the narrow road is not (p. 95). Based on your day 3 study, make your own list of what the narrow road is.
   d. Say, *Describe the woman you have always wanted to be* (p. 99).
   e. Ask members to pray. Read Romans 8:38-39 and ask them to pray this passage back to God. Remind them that God really can blow the doors off of our dreams!
4. Encourage participants to turn to the viewer guide on page 87 and take notes as they watch the video. Show video session 6.
5. Ask, *Have you laid your life on His altar? If not, lay it down and get ready to live the life Jesus dreamed for you.*
6. Play the music video, "This Is My Offering" and direct the women to the words printed on page 109. Instruct them to spend time prayerfully reading the words, listening to the music, and worshiping the Lord.

7. Close the prayer time by asking God to let this be only the beginning of your transformation—your becoming, growing, and changing into His likeness.

CELEBRATION SESSION

Before the Session

1. Recruit class members to bring refreshments.
2. View the bonus video segment, A Conversation with Angela.
3. Make a class contact list from your attendance sheet. Make enough copies for each member.

During the Session

1. Spend some time just fellowshipping as a group.
2. Show the video segment, A Conversation with Angela.
3. Open the floor for the women to share anything on their hearts regarding the study. If discussion doesn't start naturally, follow Angela's lead and ask for volunteers to share their favorite Beatitude and what makes it their favorite.
4. Close the study by thanking the participants for being so faithful to the group study and to the Lord. Pass out copies of the class contact list so members can keep up with each other now that the study is over.
5. If your group wants to continue studying together, discuss other Bible study options.*
6. Close in prayer. Thank God for your time as a group, what He has taught you, and what you have taught each other. Ask His blessings on each woman as she continues her walk with Him.

After the Final Session

Send a note to all participants, thanking them for their participation in the study. Assure them of your love and continued prayers.

* For information about other Bible study options, visit *www.lifeway.com.*

This Is My Offering

Kelly Minter • THIS IS MY OFFERING
From the album WRESTLING THE ANGELS • Cross Driven Records (2003)

I will not give what costs me nothing
When I bring my sacrifice
Cause You have asked for only one thing
That I gladly give my life
So now I lay down on Your altar
Knowing what I lose I'll find
Please receive me though I falter
For all I have is Yours, it's no longer mine

With my mouth I will praise
With my heart I will obey
This is my offering
I will go where You lead
I will trust what I can't see
This is my offering, This is my offering

May my worship be a fragrance
Rising up in sweet refrain
As I come into Your presence
May I be a life worthy of Your name

With my mouth I will praise
With my heart I will obey
This is my offering
I will go where You lead
I will trust what I can't see
This is my offering, This is my offering

Be well pleased
With my mouth I will praise
With my heart I will obey
This is my offering
I will go where You lead
I will trust what I can't see
This is my offering, This is my offering
Be well pleased

MORE TITLES *from* BEST-SELLING AUTHOR,
ANGELA THOMAS

ISBN: 0-7852-6357-8

A BEAUTIFUL OFFERING

Angela shows women that God does not require perfection, but rather our gracious obedience. This is a call for women to live their lives as grateful and beautiful offerings to the Father—imperfections, mistakes, and all!

DO YOU THINK I'M BEAUTIFUL?

Angela takes women on a deeply personal—
and deeply feminine—journey into the longing of every
woman's heart in this popular best-seller.

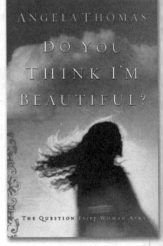

ISBN: 0-7852-6355-1

ISBN: 1-4003-0426-1

BEAUTIFUL

Angela takes the message from her best-seller *Do You Think I'm Beautiful?* and tailors it specifically for young women who will walk away confident in their newfound understanding of being beautiful through the eyes of God.

Two Ways to Earn Credit
for Studying LifeWay Christian Resources Material

CHRISTIAN GROWTH STUDY PLAN

CONTACT INFORMATION:
Christian Growth Study Plan
One LifeWay Plaza, MSN 117
Nashville, TN 37234
CGSP info line 1-800-968-5519
www.lifeway.com/CGSP
To order resources 1-800-485-2772

Christian Growth Study Plan resources are available for course credit for personal growth and church leadership training.

Courses are designed as plans for personal spiritual growth and for training current and future church leaders. To receive credit, complete the book, material, or activity. Respond to the learning activities or attend group sessions, when applicable, and show your work to your pastor, staff member, or church leader. Then go to *www.lifeway.com/CGSP,* or call the toll-free number for instructions for receiving credit and your certificate of completion.

For information about studies in the Christian Growth Study Plan, refer to the current catalog online at the CGSP Web address. This program and certificate are free LifeWay services to you.

Need a CEU?

CONTACT INFORMATION:
CEU Coordinator
One LifeWay Plaza, MSN 150
Nashville, TN 37234
Info line 1-800-968-5519
www.lifeway.com/CEU

Receive Continuing Education Units (CEUs) when you complete group Bible studies by your favorite LifeWay authors.

Some studies are approved by the Association of Christian Schools International (ACSI) for CEU credits. Do you need to renew your Christian school teaching certificate? Gather a group of teachers or neighbors and complete one of the approved studies. Then go to *www.lifeway.com/CEU* to submit a request form or to find a list of ACSI-approved LifeWay studies and conferences. Book studies must be completed in a group setting. Online courses approved for ACSI credit are also noted on the course list. The administrative cost of each CEU certificate is only $10 per course.